Curious Correlations

Party Politics and Economics

Comparing 100 Years of US Economic Performance To Political Party Control and Policies

Proposition:
"Correlation doesn't prove causation
But only a fool ignores correlation"

By Jan S. Raymond

Acknowledgments

Thanks to the following folks who played a significant part in the development of this book, although I take full responsibility for the content, including the ideas expressed and undiscovered errors in fact or computation.

Kathleen Jain - *For editing on parts of the manuscript and insightful comments.*

Baylor Odabashian - *For in depth research on economic issues and his willingness to dig deeper and raise questions that made me think carefully about exactly what I wanted to accomplish. Baylor wrote the first draft of the Chapters on Income inequality and the Housing market.*

Lloyd and Warren Kumley - *For taking the time to read the developing manuscript, make thought provoking questions and suggest ideas and edits.*

Professors Daniel Simmons and Bruce Wolk - *As my tax professors at UC Davis Law School in the late 1970's, Bruce Wolk and Daniel Simmons both exhibited great patience and respect toward students, in particular students like me with wide ranging interests beyond simply learning to practice tax law. Their patience and openness helped me develop an overall understanding of Federal Income taxation that serves me well today long after I had any professional reason for understanding tax law.*

William H. Keller and Thomas Stallard - *I started my legal career working for Bill Keller who taught that impatient young man to be patient and keep working on a problem instead of accepting a conclusion and moving on. Then Bill and his business partner Tom introduced me to the field of legislative history, which ended up being my primary business in life. The knowledge gathered in that business allowed me to recognize the patterns that led directly to this book.*

Whitney Aginaga - *For ongoing consultations on design.*

Economics Professor Michael Tansey, *Emeritus of Rockhurst University - For his detailed and thoughtful critique from the perspective of an economic professional.*

10.30.20 Edition.
Copyright 2018, 2019 - Jan S. Raymond. All rights reserved. No part of this work may be reproduced or transmitted in any form or by any means, without the written permission of the copyright holder, except as permitted by law. For permission contact Jan@naj.net, or Jan Raymond, PO Box 9216, Berkeley, CA 94707

Other Books by Jan S. Raymond
Available at Amazon Books

Fiction

Lettie

Lettie's daughter has a sudden life-threatening medical emergency that quickly becomes complicated by a terrorist threat. Lettie finds herself in a nerve-wracking psychological battle with a terrorist determined to make a bloody political statement.

Volumes in the Turmoil Series

Turmoil

Chronicles the life of Chester Turmoil, an energetic, idealistic and wealthy young entrepreneur, as he wrestles with the reality of human and political imperfection, and the complexities of relationships.

Turmoil Stories

Short background stories about Chester Turmoil's college years, political activities, and attempts to merge psychology with astrology, and efforts to create computer programs that mimic the thinking of intellectual giants of history.

Complete Turmoil

Turmoil and Turmoil Stories are combined in one volume.

Contents

1   **Prologue**
2   **Chapter 1** - A Curious Political Correlation

Section A - Philosophical Differences

6   **Chapter 2** - Economic Theory Overview
10   **Chapter 3 -** The Free Market
16   **Chapter 4** - The Size of Government
18   **Chapter 5 -** Taxation to Fund Government
19   **Chapter 6 -** The National Debt
21   **Chapter 7 -** Regulating Behavior

Section B - Historical Context

24   **Chapter 8** -Who Controlled Government - Overview
27   **Chapter 9** - Who Controlled Government - Details
29   **Chapter 10** - How We Pay for the Federal Government
33   **Chapter 11** - Overview of Tax rates since 1919
36   **Chapter 12** - Overview of the National Debt
38   **Chapter 13** - Overview of Corporations Law

Section C - Curious Correlations - Economic Data

42   **Chapter 14** – Comparing Control and GDP
45   **Chapter 15** – Comparing High Tax Rates and GDP
50   **Chapter 16** - Control, tax rates and the National Debt
55   **Chapter 17** – Control and United States Net Worth
57   **Chapter 18** - Comparing Control wand Business Formation
59   **Chapter 19** - Control and Income inequality
66   **Chapter 20**- Control and Infrastructure

Section D - Curious Correlations - Indirect Impacts

- 68 **Chapter 21** - Control and Health Care
- 71 **Chapter 22** - Control and the Housing Market
- 72 **Chapter 23** - Control and Asset Bubbles
- 75 **Chapter 24** - Control and Personal Capital
- 77 **Chapter 25** - Control and the Stock Market
- 81 **Chapter 26** - President's Party and Vocation
- 85 **Chapter 27** - Control and CEO Pay

Section E - Summary - Making Sense of the Data

- 88 **Chapter 28** - Summary of the Curious Correlations
- 90 **Chapter 29** - Understanding these Curious Correlations.
- 92 **Chapter 30** - It's Not About the People

Section F - Speculation and Ideas for Change

- 97 **Chapter 31** - Surplus Income
- 100 **Chapter 32** - How do we change the Future?
- 104 **Chapter 33** - Test Economic Opinions with Data
- 108 **Chapter 34** - Speculating on Specific Policy Changes
- 112 **Chapter 35** - Valuing These Curious Correlations

Appendices

- 115 **Appendix A** - Narrative History - Control-GDP - National Debt
- 129 **Appendix B** - Details on Tax Rates
- 134 **Appendix C** - Link to data spreadsheets
- 135 **Appendix D** - Overview - The History of Health Care in the US
- 140 **Appendix E** - Overview - Control and Housing Policy
- 148 **Appendix F** - The Authors Political Background

Prologue

This book is aimed at busy folks who don't have a lot of time to spend studying history, or economics, but want to make good decisions about voting and life. The book substitutes common language for jargon as much as possible, and aims to simplify concepts to their essence rather than trying to expound on every complication.

The goal was to develop historical and statistical fact and limit extrapolation from these facts except where extrapolation is explicit. It is intended to provide a survey of facts along with ideas that each reader can judge against their own experience.

I invite you to verify the facts and question the correlations or conclusions. To simplify your ability to check my facts I have generally relied on easily accessed public sources. Almost every source of information or computation I did not personally compile can be found quickly on the Internet. For the data I have personally compiled Appendix C contains a link to the spreadsheets from which the computations were developed.

Because our current political climate is driven by relentless partisanship, I provide in Appendix F of this volume an overview of my goals, my political background and my political views to help you judge my ability to provide an accurate reflection of data. As this book is written for lay people some economic terms with very specific meanings to economists, such as correlation, free markets and exploitation, are used in a more general common meaning sense rather in the narrower specific meaning within the economics profession. The bulk of this book was written prior to the a Covid-19 pandemic – references circumstances impacted by Covid-19 have been inserted in some locations.

Chapter 1
A Curious Political Correlation

In the general election of November of 1918, a few days before the end of World War I, the Republican Party gained majorities in both houses of Congress. They immediately began cutting taxes, cutting regulations on industry and reducing the size of Government. In 1921 the election of Republican Warren G. Harding gave Republicans control of Congress and the Presidency. Republicans controlled both the Congress and the Presidency for the next twelve (12) years.

During that twelve-year span the housing market, stock market and GDP growth initially did well. The frothy investment climate culminated In October 1929 with a crash in stock market prices, accelerating a slow-motion crash that had been developing in the housing market for four years and the US sunk into the Great Depression. Thousands of banks failed and their depositors lost their savings. Tens of thousands lost homes, farms or businesses to foreclosure. The unemployment rate rose to 25%. In the November 1932 election voters ousted Republicans and gave Democrats control of Congress and the Presidency.

In November 1994 the Republican Party again swept to a convincing electoral victory, taking substantial majorities in both houses of Congress. They immediately began cutting taxes, cutting regulations on industry and reducing the size of Government. In 2001 George W. Bush's election as President gave Republicans control of both Congress and the Presidency. Republican's controlled both houses of Congress for 12 years, and the Presidency for the last 6 of those 12 years. Over the course of those 12 years the housing market developed a speculative bubble that peaked in 2006 then collapsed into what we now call the Great Recession.

Unlike the Great Depression few people lost their savings. After the Great Depression Democrats had created an insurance system funded by Banks to prevent loss of savings due to bank failure. In addition, President Bush and President Obama followed the advice of panicked economists, who feared a second Great Depression, and bailed out big investment banks using billions of dollars of taxpayer funds to avoid a financial death spiral. But, like the Great Depression, tens of thousands of people lost their homes to foreclosure and their invested wealth to the stock market crash. The unemployment rate doubled, 8.7 million jobs disappeared and the National Debt expanded rapidly.

Here is the really curious part. In the 62 years between 1933 and 1995 Republicans only controlled both houses of Congress for 4 years (1947-1949 and 1953-1955). Democrats controlled both houses of Congress for 34 years (1933 to 1946 and 1955 to 1980). While Democrats controlled there were no economic downturns that caused problems even close to the scale of the Great Depression or Great Recession.

Historically the two worst economic collapses of the last 100 years followed the only two periods where Republicans controlled Congress for a long period of time and had free rein to cut taxes, regulations and the size of government, which they did with gusto.

How can this be? This seems so counterintuitive. Most polls show voters consider Republicans to be better at managing the economy. Is it just some weird coincidence that the two worst economic collapses in the last 100 years began at the end of the only two periods of long-term Republican control? Or does it reflect fundamental flaws in Republican economic theories?

To find out this volume develops a direct comparison between who controlled government and

GDP, the National Debt and other indicators of our economic health.

But before we can review and compare the data, we review information to help us make sense of whatever findings we turn up. We review free market theory – how an economy is supposed to work; the ideological differences between Republicans and Democrats and the historical political context in which the last 100 years played out.

Section A

Market Theory and Philosophical Differences

    Chapter 2 – Economic Theory Overview

    Chapter 3 - The Free Market

    Chapter 4 - The Size of Government

    Chapter 5 - Taxation to Fund Government

    Chapter 6 - The National Debt

    Chapter 7 - Regulating Behavior

Chapter 2

Economic Theory Overview

Before we can begin discussing philosophical differences between Republicans and Democrats, we first need to review some basic economic concepts so we can understand if the ideological differences between Republicans and Democrats matter.

1. **Free Market Theory** - Capitalism, free market theory, socialism and communism are philosophical theories developed by thinkers with a focus on economics rather than broader focus on, for example, the purpose of life. People use these economic generalizations to simplify day-to-day decision-making.

2. **The distinction between trade and growth.** Free Market theory is about how people connect up to engage in trade. But trade in itself does not produce new value. If Dick has a lot of apples, and Jane has a lot of oranges they may trade apples for oranges. Wealth was created when Dick and Jane cultivated the orchard and harvested the apples and oranges. But no wealth is created when they trade apples for oranges. What trade does is encourage people to develop more wealth. Without trade once Dick has enough apples for his personal use, he has no reason to cultivate more. Trade motivates Dick to create more wealth than he can personally use so he can trade for other items he does not have.

We don't barter much these days. Modern economies rely on the circulation of money rather than direct barter of one item for another item. Money allows Anne, who is selling a car, to trade with Dick. Anne doesn't want a barn full of apples in exchange for her car. Money makes trade easy by allowing Dick the apple seller to accumulate money from lots of people buying apples so he can buy a car from one person.

3. **Capital** - Economists and politicians tend to elevate the word "Capital" to something mysterious that is beyond the understanding of mortal humans. But it simply means is you have some spare wealth stuck away that is not being used up by life expenses. That spare wealth is your capital. It can be money, assets or even a skill you possess. As we go about life, we gather property such as clothes, houses, cars, jewelry and money. If we have extra property, we may decide to protect it for future trade or convert it to money we can use to generate more wealth. We are investing our capital.

4. **Investments that Create Wealth** - Political arguments seldom (in my experience never) distinguish between investments that create new wealth, and investments that are simply trade that reallocates a bit of existing wealth to the value of an asset. Here are some simple examples to illustrate these basic distinctions.

If you take your spare money and buy undeveloped land you are not creating new wealth, you are reallocating a little bit of existing wealth to the value of that land that is exactly as it was before you bought it.

If you take your spare money and buy another house in your neighborhood to rent out for income you are still not creating new wealth. It is simply bumping up the price of an existing asset a little bit, in essence reallocating a little of the value of existing wealth to that asset. The rent you receive may make you personally wealthier but is not a net gain in wealth for society.

If you take the money you have laying about, buy a bunch of building materials, hire some people and build a house you have created new value that adds to the stock of existing wealth.

If you use your spare money to buy stock from some other investor who owns the stock, you have created nothing new, you have simply reallocated a little bit of existing wealth to the price of that stock. If you buy stock from a new company raising money to develop a new service or product you may be facilitating the creation of new wealth.

If you loan money to someone who is using it to buy existing buildings, or play the stock market, that loaned money is not creating new wealth, it is facilitating the reallocation of existing wealth.

5. Personal skills as Capital - Each of us may develop skills that have value in our life. This form of capital, in terms of our distinction between transactions that create new wealth and transactions that simply reallocate the value of existing assets, follows roughly the same course as property capital. If your skill is as a financial analyst your skill is probably seldom creating new wealth, you are simply skilled at reallocating wealth. If you are a contractor building structures, or businessman building a business you are creating new wealth in your efforts.

The real world is much more complex. When you buy bare land, or a house, or stock, the money you transfer to the seller may, or may not, be invested in something that creates new wealth. Even a financial expert may sometimes create value by facilitating new wealth creation. But understanding this basic distinction between investments that create new wealth and investments that simply reallocate wealth is crucial to trying to understand how to make the free market as productive as possible, by not mistaking trade for wealth creation.

6.   Key motivations important to market functioning. There are many motivations that bring people into a market place, to be discussed further in the following chapter. But two particular personality types determine whether a market grows or stagnates - entrepreneurs and empire builders.

Entrepreneurs, people motivated by finding new, more efficient ways to accomplish work, are a huge benefit to any market. Their ideas may sometimes be a little crazy, but even their bad ideas generate activity in the market and their good ideas make the world a little richer.

Empire builders, people motivated to cultivate personal wealth and power, have mixed impacts on markets. Their drive and energy are a major benefit as they organize and push business development. But their focus on their own wealth and power, if not constrained by the large society, will tend to impoverish the overall society as wealth and power get concentrated in a few individuals. In effect they undermine market growth by undermining the consumer base that supports a diverse economy.

We are now ready to look at the ideological differences between Republicans and Democrats.

Chapter 3
The Free Market

In economic matters both Republicans and Democrats broadly support a free market economy so our inquiry begins by identifying the characteristics of a free market where Republicans and Democrats have different views.

As used in this volume the term free market refers to a market where individuals control their own economic activities. A free market is arguably the natural state of human interaction in the absence of government. It is akin to natural selection in animal species. In its raw form the individuals who are most adapted to the environment, or lucky, survive and thrive. The poorly adapted, or unlucky, get exploited or go extinct.

Free markets did not develop as a specific philosophical choice. They were simply a starting point for organized human society. Economists speak of the market as guided by "the invisible hand." The theory is our basic behavioral tendencies strike a balance between competing interests. For example, in theory as the unemployment rate drops, wages should rise as workers become more in demand. No need for Government to do anything according to the "invisible hand" theory.

A free markets basic advantage is that it allows individuals to pursue what they see as their best interest. The clever and innovative can innovate. The hard working can advance their interests by working hard. The thrifty can build up a nest egg.

An unregulated free market has two basic disadvantages.

Speculation - A free market often invites (and rewards) speculation. Speculation is trading to garner wealth without producing a good or service. Speculation can serve useful purposes. A speculator may buy some asset from someone else anticipating it will increase in value, which provides wealth to the seller to use for other purposes that may create some asset or service. Speculation plays a key role in funding enterprise. But speculation has a history of becoming a liability as speculators take bigger and bigger risks looking for a payday and eventually cause major disruption in the economy.

Exploitation - The second, and more serious downside of the unregulated free market is clever or powerful people may find a way to exploit the weakness or vulnerability of others. They can exploit through poorly compensated labor, or through clever manipulation or application of the law, or through excessive exploitation of the environment that we all share, or through use of knowledge denied to others. Exploitation is a recipe for an unstable society that leaves a lot of people unhappy, angry and potentially violent.

The Race to the Bottom - Economists speak of the race to the bottom when exploitation allows a business to produce a particular good or service at a lower cost than competitors not exploiting. As an extreme example a business using uncompensated slaves for labor will have vastly lower costs of production than a business competitor paying wages to workers. A competing business not relying on slave labor cannot survive, as their prices need to be much higher to cover the cost of wages. The non-exploiting business then has to either get out of the business or hold their nose and adopt the exploitative practices to be competitive. In effect the free market rewards selfish behavior oblivious to the effect on other persons.

This free market race to the bottom often characterized the United States economy in the first 150 years after the birth of the nation and we are still dealing with the backwash. Our most revered founding father, George Washington, owed his financial independence to slavery. His many slaves worked his vast landholdings. He spoke of being uncomfortable about slavery but felt hemmed in by the slave-based economy in which he lived. He felt he couldn't unilaterally free his slaves without going bankrupt.[1]

Thomas Jefferson, the man who wrote the immortal words that have come to epitomize our aspiration toward freedom - *"We hold these truths to be self-evident: that all men are created equal; that they are endowed by their Creator with certain unalienable rights; that among these are life, liberty, and the pursuit of happiness."* was also a slaveholder and also spoke of feeling constrained and unhappy about the same market forces as Washington.[2]

Washington and Jefferson both argued that the economics of slavery would eventually end slavery. Instead it nearly killed our country through Civil War. Exploitation is like an addictive drug. It is extremely difficult for those in the position of being able to exploit to voluntarily give up their power, so exploitation generally survives until overturned by extreme social unrest.

Not to suggest the Southern Slave states had a corner on the exploitation market when the Civil War occurred. The Northern States won the war due to their industrial capacity. But workers in those Northern

---

[1] "Washington, A Life", Ron Chernow, Penguin Books, 2010, p.799 to 804
[2] "Thomas Jefferson, The Art of Power", Jon Meacham, Random House, 2012, p.474 to 478.

factories worked horrendous hours, under dangerous conditions, for little pay. Even 40 years after the end of the Civil War some workers at US Steel worked seven days a week, 12-hour days and, once every two weeks, a 24-hour day.[3] At best a short step above slavery. The political argument that finally gave the anti-slavery position the political muscle to elect anti-slavery politicians like Abraham Lincoln wasn't the moral argument against slavery. It was the argument directed to white working men that slavery depressed wages for all working people.[4]

Free markets create benefits to us all as they produce clever new ways of doing things. But once knowledge becomes widespread the market tends to devolve into a race to the bottom where the firms that exploit other people, or the environment we all share, force others in the same business to exploit to survive.

It would seem sensible that government should take the role of encouraging the positive behaviors that drive the free market while preventing exploitation by establishing minimum standards to protect workers, consumers and the environment to which all the businesses in a market must abide.

The economic differences between Republicans and Democrats arise in how the parties view the different types of behaviors that drive participants in our free market. Looking at the five categories we have identified we find:

Innovation - The push to find faster, or more efficient, or more cost-effective ways to accomplish

---

[3] "The Forgotten Depression - 1921: The Crash that Cured itself", James Grant, Simon and Schuster Paperbacks, 2014, p. 157.
[4] See generally the Wikipedia page on "Abolitionism in the United States" and also generally, "A Self Made Man - The Political Life of Abraham Lincoln", Sidney Blumenthal, Simon and Schuster Paperbacks, 2016, and in particular discussion at p. 453.

things we already do, or create things that improve our lives. Everybody loves innovators.

Making a living - Doing what we need to do to provide food, shelter and clothe and amuse ourselves. Both parties generally celebrate the virtues of hard work.

Saving - Both parties also encourage folks desire to store some wealth in assets that hold value.

Speculation - Using accumulated (or borrowed) wealth to accumulate more through clever manipulation of wealth. Republicans virtually always support any sort of speculation. Democrats are somewhat more suspicious, particularly of speculation with another person's money.

Exploitation - Republicans are tolerant of building wealth by exploiting the labor of others, or exploiting the world we share (the commons) to the detriment of others, or manipulating the law to gain a market advantage. Republicans assume it is economically necessary. Democrats tend to view all exploitation as bad.

Innovation, making a living and saving are motivations that tend to not directly impact other market participants. On the other hand, speculation and exploitation always involve other market participants. Any speculation or exploitation creates potential conflict.

No political party has a monopoly on any particular motivation. All of us at some point in life consider or engage in behavior motivated by each of these five behavioral paths. They are natural alternatives in our thought processes bequeathed by the structure of our brain. But politicians seeking votes construct ideologies that favor particular attitudes toward these motivations. The ideologies over time can become divorced from current reality. It is these ideologies that we seek to compare.

Now we are ready to look at what each party states to be their philosophy about the size of government, taxes to support government, government debt, and regulation of individual conduct by government.

As we review what each party states as its philosophical view of governing, we will, when pertinent, note which behaviors each party philosophy seems to emphasize, or de-emphasize.

Chapter 4
The Size of Government

"Less Government in Business and More Business in Government" - Warren G. Harding.

"The Business of America is Business"
Calvin Coolidge.

"The test of our progress is not whether we add more to the abundance of those who have much it is whether we provide enough for those who have little."

Franklin D. Roosevelt.

These quotes from three Presidents, two Republicans from the 1920's Republican domination that ended in the Great Depression, and the Democrat who took over in 1933 in the depths of that Great Depression, demonstrate the primary historical philosophical difference between Republicans and Democrats.

Republicans believe business can do everything better than Government. Republicans think the motivations that lead people to generate wealth for themselves are largely irrelevant as government intervention will do more harm than good. Republicans tend to be supportive of any form of speculation and reluctant to allow government to address exploitation.

The opposite of the Republican philosophy would be Socialism or Communism, both rooted in the idea that Government does everything better than private business. Although occasionally a Socialist has been elected, this idea has never been a significant force in American politics. Democrats (at least the ones that get elected) accept that the free market is the best economic system for most human endeavors, but believe government is necessary to mitigate business excesses through regulation to prevent the tendency of a free market to push business into a race to the bottom. Democrats are more suspicious of speculation (particularly with borrowed money) and have often acted to moderate or prevent exploitation.

Chapter 5

Taxation to Fund Government

It is a rare politician, Republican or Democrat, who will publicly advocate raising taxes and many will readily say they are for lower taxes. But the philosophy of each party dictates the attitudes on taxation they will act on.

Since Republicans believe business can do everything better than government cutting taxes and freeing up business is always the goal. Republicans have virtually always campaigned on lowering taxes, and followed through on their promises when given the power to act.

Democrats believe government is necessary to mitigate the markets tendency toward a race to the bottom. Regulation by government is necessary to prevent excessive speculation or exploitation and to mitigate the hardship on those left behind. Regulation costs money, so it is appropriate to tax to cover the costs.

Chapter 6

The National Debt

We begin by distinguishing between the deficit and the debt. The deficit refers to the difference between government income and expenditures in a given year. The national debt is a measure of the total accumulated government debt. We focus on the national debt in this volume.

Like higher taxes, it is rare for a politician of either party to urge an increase in the National debt. But the fundamental philosophical differences between Republicans and Democrats result in significant differences in their approach to the national debt - which spring directly from their views on government and taxes. However, in some respects Republicans have switched positions on the National Debt over the last 100 years.

After World War I ended the US went through a frantic inflationary boom for a year and a half or so then flipped into a rapid, deep depression. By early 1922 many of the soldiers who had fought in the War were experiencing unemployment and hard times, and military pay during and after the war had not kept pace with inflation. In the fall of 1922, the Republican Congress sent Republican President Harding a soldier's bonus bill to compensate veterans to help them deal with the difficult economic times. 38 states had already enacted bonus bills. President Harding vetoed the bill citing the need to reduce the national debt.[5] (A version of the bill was passed two years later over Republican President Coolidge's veto).

---

[5] "The Forgotten Depression - 1921: The Crash that Cured itself", James Grant, Simon and Schuster Paperbacks, 2014, p. 138 to. 141.

Since Ronald Reagan however Republicans have made increased defense spending a cornerstone of their economic platform, along with tax cuts with little concern for increases in the National Debt.

For Reagan Republicans taxes reduce the money available for private enterprise so the best policy is to cut taxes whenever possible because in the end the free market will do a better job of taking care of people than government. If you cannot cut government spending because we are at war, or preparing for war, or because Democrats won't agree to eliminate some program, tax cuts are more important than a balanced budget. Reagan Republicans also believe that increased government spending on defense will be offset by increased revenues from spending by the folks with more money in their pocket from tax cuts so no net increase in the national debt will occur.

Democrats believe that government should smooth off the rough edges of the free market with social programs to assist the least fortunate that cost money. Democrats have regularly proposed and passed programs they deem to be good for the country which expand the overall size of government. But unlike Republicans Democrats have no ideological antipathy to raising taxes. Democrats, if given the chance, historically have paid for programs even if it requires an increase in tax revenues.

Chapter 7

Regulating Behavior

It would seem that in a free country government's primary domestic policy function should be as essentially an arbitrator or mediator. When an individual engages in behavior that has no impact on others it should not be governments business. On the other hand, when an individual engages in behavior that has a direct impact on a broader community, government should step in to set up rules to protect the community from negative consequences while allowing the individual as much freedom as is consistent with the community interest.

With that preface we look at the historical philosophical differences between Republicans and Democrats.

Regulating Market Behavior - Since Republicans believe business does everything better than government, they are disinclined to regulate behavior in the marketplace. They do not draw distinctions between the motivations that drive people to make money, so they pay little attention to controlling speculation or exploitation, even though these market activities almost by definition affect the broader community.

Democrats have historically been more aggressive about regulating market activities, providing curbs on speculation and attempting to ameliorate exploitation.

Regulating Personal Behavior - Republicans have historically been inclined toward regulating freedom in personal choices that strike Republicans as wrongheaded by criminalizing private conduct. In the last 100 years Republicans have largely driven the war on drugs in its various iterations, from its beginnings in the 1920's through the recent string of Republican Presidents who created the terminology "war" on drugs. Republicans in the last 50 years have often proposed using law to deny civil rights based on sex or personal sexual behavior and followed through if elected.

Democrats are more protective of an individual's right to make non-economic choices about how to lead their life as long as those choices don't have a significant impact on their community. In criminalizing drug and alcohol consumption they have been followers rather than leaders, usually arguing we should treat drug use as a medical or psychological issue that should be treated.

Democrats, on the other hand, have taken the lead in Civil Rights in the last 50 years, pushing for laws governing discrimination on the basis of race, gender, sexual orientation or other personal characteristics or choices that do not directly impact others. That was not the case from the 1920's to the late 1960's when the south was solidly Democrat. The Democrats taking the lead in pushing for Civil rights is probably the most obvious reason the south switched from solidly Democrat to solidly Republican leading to the Republican domination from 1981 to the present.

Many Republicans are uncomfortable with addressing Civil Rights, given that party became a national power under Abraham Lincoln seeking to abolish slavery. Since 1970 Republicans have needed the votes of the south for their economic and military agenda. In the same way many Democrats went along with the drug war to get elected, many Republicans have taken anti-civil rights positions to get in a position to accomplish the economic and foreign policy goals they regard as higher priority.

Section B - Historical Context

Chapter 8 - Who Controlled Government - Overview
Chapter 9 - Who Controlled Government - Details
Chapter 10 - How We Pay for the Federal Government
Chapter 11 - Overview of Tax rates since 1919
Chapter 12 - Overview of the National Debt
Chapter 13 - Overview of Corporations Law

Chapter 8
Who Controlled Government - Overview

In order to compare the impact of political ideology on economics we first must find a way to assign economic data to one party or the other for the periods that party controlled policy.

To create a system of comparison we begin with some basic high school civics facts. A defining characteristic of the United States Government is our three separate but equal branches of Government. The Executive Branch, the Legislative Branch and the Judiciary are deemed three equal powers.

However, only the Executive and the Legislative branch, the two branches elected by voters, have the power to enact law. The Judicial Branch functions as a check on the power of the Executive and Legislative branches enacting law that contradicts the constitution, or other law.

This volume will focus on which party controlled the elective power centers, the President, the Senate and the House of Representatives. Direct comparison between Republicans and Democrats is facilitated by the fact that, despite a plethora of smaller parties over the years, no party other than the Democrats or the Republicans controlled any of these three elective centers of power in the last 100 years.[6]

---

[6] See Appendix C for links to spreadsheets. Sitting down with the Federal Statutes for each two-year session and manually counting the party representatives for each party was method for compiling the Congressional portion of this chart. When the Senate is tied control is awarded to the Presidents party as the Vice-President has the

Since in every two-year congressional session that occurred between 1919 and 2018 either Republicans or Democrats controlled at least two of these three elective power centers this approach offers a unique opportunity to compare how the country did when Republicans were in control compared to when Democrats were in control. An opportunity to compare party control to GDP growth, to rise or fall of the National debt, to how party policy preferences affected infrastructure, the housing market, the stock market, or income distribution.

First, we distinguish between two types of control. **Complete control** when one party controls both houses of Congress and the Presidency, or **majority control** - one party controlling two of the three elective power centers. Historically no big changes in policy direction occur in the absence of long-term complete control by one party. Big changes in policy tend to occur when one party controls all three centers of power for an extended period of time until the other party gains a similar dominance for a long period of time.

Going back in time reliable data is sparse for the some of the economic data comparison requires. But changes in technology have also made life in the modern United States fundamentally different from life pre-World War I. This volume will focus on economic comparisons for the period after the major technological innovations driven by World War I when a new Congress began in March of 1919 through the end of the Congressional session of 2017-2018.

Two slightly different forms of control will be also compared to reflect the fact that when one party is dominant over a long period of time, there are often short

---

deciding vote.

interludes when the other party briefly gains complete control.

The term **Control** will be used to refer to actual control of ⅔ of the elective power for each of the 50 two-year Congressional Sessions in the last 100 years. One or the other of the two parties enjoyed complete controlled in 56 of the last 100 years. In the other 44 years one party maintained majority control.

The words **Policy dominance** will refer to periods of time when one party's policy preference dominated for a long period of time, although control, both complete and majority, may have switched for brief periods of time during the overall period of policy dominance.

Chapter 9
Who Controlled Government – Details

Although reliable historical data for the period before 1919 is spotty, a brief overview of the 60 years prior to 1919 provides interesting context beginning at the point the Republican Party became a political force in opposition to the then existing Democratic Party.[7]

From 1859 to 1918 Republican policy dominated government all but a few years. In the 30 Congressional Sessions over that 60-year span Republicans had a controlling majority in the Senate in 23 of the 30 sessions, a controlling majority in the House in 19 of the 30 and we had Republican Presidents for 20 of the 30 sessions of Congress. Republicans had complete control during fourteen (14) of those 30 sessions, Democrats three (3).

History suggests the only reason the Democrats occasionally briefly grabbed complete control resulted from a steady string of financial collapses during that 60 years. Republicans controlled Congress from 1859 to 1875 with a Republican President in 10 of those 16 years (1861 to 1865 and 1869 to 1875). Republican Presidents were in office the entire period from 1869 to 1885. But a financial collapse in 1873 provided an opening for the Democrats to take control of the House in 1875 and add the Senate in 1879. Republicans regained control of the House and Senate in 1881 but lost the House in 1883, shortly before a financial collapse in 1884. For the next four years Congress remained divided with a Democratic President. In 1889 Republicans regained control of the House, the Senate and the Presidency. A financial crash

---

[7] Information drawn from *"The Forgotten Depression - 1921: The Crash That Cured Itself"* by James Grant, Simon and Schuster paperback and Wikipedia links regarding *Party divisions of United States Congresses* and *List of Presidents of the United States*.

in 1890 allowed the Democrats to regain control of the House in 1891 and control both the House and Senate in 1893, with a Democratic President. In 1895 Republicans regained both the House and the Senate, although with a Democratic President. In 1897 a Republican President took office and Republicans held control of all three elective power centers until 1911 - despite financial collapses in 1903, 1907 and 1910. A financial collapse in 1913 coincided with Democrats taking control of all three centers of power with Woodrow Wilson as President. The Republicans took back the House as we formally entered World War I in 1917.

With that lead-in of Republican domination punctuated by financial collapses established, we do a quick overview of who controlled government in the last 100 years:

1919 through 2018 Overview

Democrats controlled for 58 of the last 100 years

They controlled the Presidency, House and Senate in 34 years. A Democratic Congress negotiated with a Republican President in 20 years. A Democratic President negotiated with a split Congress in 4 years

Republicans controlled for 42 of the last 100 years.

They controlled the Presidency, House and Senate for 22 years. A Republican Congress negotiated with a Democratic President for 14 years. A Republican President negotiated with a split Congress for 6 years.

Appendix A contains a narrative detailed historical overview of who controlled government the last 100 years, and spreadsheets you can link to from Appendix C.

Chapter 10
How We Pay for the Federal Government

A Curious Fact: The National Debt, now about 22 Trillion dollars, is frequently blamed on Social Security or other "entitlement" programs. Factually entitlement programs like Social Security, unemployment insurance and Medicare are funded by the payroll tax, money collected from workers and employers and kept in separate trust fund accounts. The payroll tax funds have never run a deficit. About 12% of the National Debt is actually payroll tax proceeds Congress "borrowed" in the last thirty years to fund government so they would not have to raise income taxes.

Despite the claims of some politicians the 22 billion-dollar national debt is entirely a function of Congress not raising enough money through the income tax to pay for defense and government operations.

Overview of Taxation - To make sense of the economic performance under the two parties we first review tax policy and how it impacts Federal government finances. Although there are many different ways our Government raises money from citizens, the vast bulk of the money comes from either **Income Taxes** or **Payroll taxes**. Because of some curious correlations with GDP data we also include some background on Federal inheritance taxes although they have always been a relatively small contributor to the Federal Government finances.

Income Tax: This tax is computed on each taxpayer's annual income. The amount of tax depends on how much you make each year. Not all income is treated the same. In our modern system generally (and perhaps counter intuitively) those working for wages often pay a higher tax rate than those who are (figuratively) sitting back and letting the money roll in from investments. Since 1921 the rate of tax on passive income (investments paying Capital Gains) has usually been less than the rate of tax applied to many taxpayers on their income tax from working.

The Income tax is a graduated tax system. To help understand what this means we will look at the original 1913 tax law that enacted the modern income tax. The law provided seven tax brackets, which we list in the chart below. *Keep in mind these dollar amounts represent the taxpayer's **income for the year**, not their net wealth.* To make it easier to relate this discussion to modern experience all dollar amounts have been converted to show the approximate amount it correlates to in 2018 dollars.[8]

Annual Income (1913 dollars)	2018 value	Tax rate
Up to $3000 ($4000 married)	$66,000 ($88,000)	0
Over $3000 up to $20,000	$500,000	1%.
Over $20,000 but less than $50,000	$1.25 million	2%.
Over $50,000 but less than $75,000	$1.9 million	3%
Over $75,000 but less than $100,000	$2.5 million	4%
Over $100,000 but less than $250,000	$6.2 million	5%
Over $250,000 but less than $500,000	$12.5 million	6%
Over $500,000	$12.5 million +	7%.

What does the Income Tax Fund: The money that is derived from Federal Income Tax covers most of the costs of running the Federal Government. Currently fifty cents ($.50) of every dollar of income tax collected is spent on defense. The remaining 50% is allocated to cover all the other cost of running the Federal

---

[8] Computed using https://www.carinsurancedata.org/calculators/inflation

Government. Funding for the Executive Branch, Federal agencies, the Congress, the Federal Courts, disaster relief, infrastructure projects - it is all almost exclusively funded by the Income Tax.

Payroll Tax: Your employer takes payroll taxes directly out of your paycheck, or if you are self employed you pay your payroll taxes along with your income taxes. Unlike income taxes you only pay Payroll taxes on income up to a set ceiling ($127,000 in 2017).[9] You don't pay any payroll taxes on the amounts you make in a year that exceed the set ceiling. The payroll tax is completely funded by wages on working people who pay taxes on every dollar they make, or interest on the funds accumulated in the payroll tax trust fund. The funds generated from payroll taxes are (in theory) set aside to be used only for specific programs benefiting workers who paid the taxes including Social Security, unemployment insurance and other programs for the protection of workers (Medicare is partially funded by payroll taxes but supplementary funding comes from other sources of federal income).

As noted above this distinction between the Income Tax and the Payroll Tax is crucial to understanding the Federal Budget Deficit and the National Debt. The Payroll tax proceeds are deposited in trust funds that in theory cannot be used for other purposes. The Payroll Tax trust funds have **always** run surpluses - to date expenditures have never been more than the taxes collected. The National Debt is a function of the failure of the Government to collect enough income taxes to cover the cost of defense and Government administration. Part of our National debt (somewhere around $3 to 4 trillion) reflects Congress in

---

[9] See this Motley Fool article for general discussion.
https://www.fool.com/retirement/2017/01/28/81-years-of-social-securitys-maximum-taxable-earni.aspx

the last 30 years "borrowing" from the payroll tax trust funds to cover the cost of defense and government operations. In effect a double tax on lower income folks who pay payroll taxes - they now are on the hook to pay interest on a part of the national debt that is their own money.

The Inheritance Tax (officially the Estate Tax) on the other hand is only paid by persons wealthy enough to pass on millions to their heirs. If when you die you leave property valued above a certain value, you owe a percentage of that value to the Government. The more you leave, the higher the percentage the Government taxes.

The current Estate Tax was enacted in 1916 in response to a loss of tariff income during World War I. In 1916 you were exempt from the tax unless you left property whose value exceeded (in 2003 dollars) $11,000,000. Anything over $11,000,000 but below the next bracket threshold was taxed at the rate of 1%. The highest bracket taxed you at 10% on the parts of your estate exceeding $1 Billion (2003 dollars).[10]

---

[10] Heritage Foundation Backgrounder No. 1719, January 16, 2004, "Estate Taxes - A Historical Perspective", January 16 2004.

Chapter 11
Overview of Tax Rates Since 1919
Income, Payroll and Inheritance Taxes

We pay particular attention to tax rates as they offer perhaps the most objectively simple comparison of how differences between Republican and Democratic ideological views are expressed in legislative activity.

Curious Fact: - When Republicans control government tax rates on wealthy taxpayers drop and when Democrats control government tax rates on wealthy taxpayers rise.

1919 to 1932 - Republicans controlled policy and the highest income tax rates dropped from 73% to 25%. Inheritance Tax rates from 1919 to 1932 fluctuated but in 1932 a top rate of 40% applied to the wealthiest taxpayers.[11]

1933 to 1981 - Democrats controlled policy and the highest income tax rates rose from 25% to over 90% then dropped to 70%. Estate Tax rates on the wealthiest taxpayers went up to 70%, then to 80% then back down to 70%.

1982 to the present - Republicans controlled policy and the highest income tax rates dropped from 70% to below 40%. The highest Estate Tax rate dropped from 70% to about 65% and has remained at that level.

Details

[11] General references for the Estate Tax: Wikipedia - "Estate tax in the United States - History and heritage.org/taxes/report/estate-taxes-historical-perspective

Tax law is astonishing in its convoluted complexity. At any point in time the actual tax any one individual must pay may be affected by hundreds - perhaps thousands of possible deductions, credits, offsets, interpretations or other factors. In this brief discussion we seek simple numbers broadly representative of the trend rather than attempting to identify the ever-changing factors that create the devilish details.

Special note - Capital Gains taxation - Passive investment income (income derived from the sale of property other than goods you manufacture for sale such as selling stock or some other asset) was originally treated like all other income in 1913. A special tax bracket for Capital Gains was created in 1923 and Capital Gain has been treated differently than wage income ever since, drawing different distinctions according to how long you held an asset, or other factors as it has evolved. On the following page we provide a representative figure to demonstrate the trend in taxation, without trying to keep track of the exclusions, exemptions and variations.

A curious fact - over the last 100 years the percentage of taxpayers paying a higher tax rate on wages than are paid on passive investment income has steadily increased to the point the tax rate on Capital Gain is lower than the tax rate applicable to wages for all but the poorest taxpayers.

Overview of the history of the top income tax rate on wages and Capital Gains since 1919:

Time Period	Top wage tax bracket	Capital Gain
1918	War time rate peaked at 77%	N/A
1919 to 1931	Drops from 73% to 25%	12.5%
1932 to 1945	Rises to over 90%	25%
1945 to 1963	Stays over 90%	25%
1964 to 1981	Over 70%	28%
1982 to 1986	50%	28%
1987 to present	Below 40%	20%

Chapter 12
Overview of the National Debt

Curious Fact - The National Debt dropped continuously from right after World War II when it topped out at 116% of GDP to a little over 30% of GDP in 1980. Since 1981 it has risen to current estimates of about 108% of GDP. Why, after dropping for over 30 years did it then grow for the next 38 years?

Details - Historically war has been the primary driver of the National debt. Our National debt began with the Revolutionary War. At the end of the Revolutionary War as a country we owed an amount equal to 30% of the economic value the entire country generated in a year (the figure economists today call Gross Domestic Product, or GDP). For the next 75 or so years the US National debt generally fell steadily although we had war expenses from time to time. By 1860 the National Debt was under 5% of GDP. The Civil War fueled a jump to near 40% of GDP in half a decade.

After the Civil War the debt dropped back down to under 5% of GDP by the early 1900's. World War I drove the debt back up to near 40% of GDP by the time the war ended in 1918.

With the end of World War I in November 1918 Government immediately began scaling back expenditures as the military demobilized so the federal budget began to shrink. In 1919 the US had a balanced budget, but a national debt amounting to 35% of GDP. The Debt dropped to around 20% of GDP by the time of the stock market crash of 1929.

In 1930 the National debt began to rise rapidly due to the collapse in tax revenue from lower tax rates and the inability of Government to stop the slide into the Great Depression. By 1940 the debt was again over 40% of GDP. After Pearl Harbor on December 7, 1941 the country went into full war mobilization. Both the Federal budget deficit and the National Debt surged higher. By the end of World War II the National Debt was 116% of GDP, that is to say we owed more than we produced in a full year.

Between 1945 and 1980 the National Debt shrunk from 116% of GDP to about 30% of GDP.

Ronald Reagan's election in 1980 was a turning point for the National Debt. By the end of the Reagan years the National debt was nearing 50% of GDP. Since then it has continued rising, accelerating the increase after the Great Recession hit and currently stands above 100% of GDP, once again we owe more than we produce in a full year.

Chapter 13

Overview of Corporations Law

Our last item for historical context is a quick look at business corporations. Corporations dominate our economy, but corporations are not a natural result of a free market. They are in fact the most prevalent form of government intervention in free markets.

Corporations solve a basic problem in human nature. Here is an example that illuminates the problem:

Enterprising Ed owns a house on a small farm, and a small manufacturing facility in town. Ed has managed his holdings well and finds he has the time and wealth to expand into some new business venture. Ed's net worth is $1,000,000.

Ed borrows $200,000 to buy a boat so he can ship his goods to other markets, and also make money shipping other folk's goods.

Ed does a good job of marketing his shipping services so his first voyage departs with $800,000 worth of goods besides his own. However, an unexpected storm at sea sinks his new boat and all is lost. Ed lost his boat he owes $200,000 on and the people who owned the goods Ed was shipping sue to recover their $800,000 in lost goods. Ed is financially ruined.

Ed's neighbors take a lesson from Ed's bad luck. When they have wealth beyond what they need they do not get tempted to try starting some risky new venture - even if it offers big profits. They do not want to put all their wealth at risk so they invest cautiously in fixed assets that they can control and that will hold their value, such as gold, or land.

President Sam, who runs the country in which Ed lives, sees more and more people stashing extra wealth in safe fixed assets. There is little new business to provide jobs and growth. Sam realizes he needs to do something if he wants to keep his job. How does Sam encourage the people who hold wealth to be bold in investing in new ventures? How can you allow people to invest in risky enterprises while not risking losing all their wealth?

The corporation is the modern answer. Government passes laws that set up rules that, if followed carefully, allow investors with an idea to set up a Corporation where the only money an investor risks is the wealth the investor transfers to the Corporation. The liability for catastrophic loss lies with the Corporation.

Historically corporations did not become the major feature of the US economy until the 19th century as the Industrial Revolution required bigger and bigger investments (and risks) to put new technology to work. As corporations became dominant Government started to see them as a revenue source. As a result, corporations are subject to the same race to the bottom forces that plague an unfettered free market. In the United States individual states have the authority to authorize the formation of corporations and set the rules for corporations within their state. States competing for the right to tax corporations have often done so by seeking to attract corporations with lenient rules that favor the interests of folks who set up corporations with little regard toward the public interest in individual accountability and honesty. The most lenient states limit the ability of other states to protect the public interest since incorporators will simply go off to another more accommodating state to incorporate. Although there are few good reasons to allow a corporation to own an interest in another corporation, many parts of modern economies are dominated by impenetrable thickets of stacked corporations to mask ownership and avoid tax liabilities.

At the federal level the first corporate income tax was enacted in 1894 and corporate income taxes have been a cornerstone of the US Tax system ever since. However, corporations are hard to tax. Their ability to shape the rules that govern them make them adept at getting special favors out of Congress, and they can set up a complex web of subsidiary corporations to manage, or even hide wealth. As of 2010 about 9% of Federal Revenues came from corporate income taxes.

Taxing the income of corporations is not particularly logical if our goal is to foster risk taking. We create corporations to encourage people to invest funds in risky enterprises. If we tax corporate profits, we are effectively pulling money out of the risk pool. It would seem to make more sense to tax the money coming out of corporations than to tax wealth being held in corporations.

Section C

Curious Correlations - Economic Data

Chapter 14 - Control and GDP

Chapter 15 - Tax Rates and GDP

Chapter 16 - Control, tax rates and the National Debt

Chapter 17 - Control and United States Net Worth

Chapter 18 - Control and Business Formation

Chapter 19 - Control and Income inequality

Chapter 20 - Control and Infrastructure

Chapter 14
Comparing Control and GDP

The bulk of this data is derived from computations of relatively complex data, not interesting for many folks. Rather than have you yawn and put the book down, and maybe never get back to it, we begin with a summary of the findings that are the core of this chapter. The details can be found in spreadsheets and narratives set forth in the Appendices.

Chapter Summary - Curiously the public perception that Republicans are better at managing the economy is backwards, according to the GDP growth of the US economy by year over the last 100 years. Correlating GDP with which party controls ⅔ or all three elective power centers we find:

> **In 58 years of Democratic control
> GDP growth averaged 2.9%.**
>
> **In 42 years of Republican control
> GDP growth averaged 1%.**[12]

We use the two computations, although both produce similar results. First comparing control with GDP for each year of actual control. Second, we compute with a one-year offset. Since any new Congress will be acting in an environment shaped by past decisions they may initially look better or worse than they deserve. So, we skip the year they take over, but

---

[12] We include as Appendix C a link to spreadsheets demonstrating the computations these figures are based upon.

give them credit (or blame) for the year the following Congress is seated.

When one party controls the House, Senate and Presidency: Republicans have produced a per year growth in GDP that averages 0.3%. Democrats have produced a per year growth in GDP that averages 3.8%.

When one party controls the Presidency, and one house of Congress: With a Republican President and Republican control of one house GDP growth averages 2.28% per year. With a Democratic Presidents and Democratic control of one house GDP averages 2.02% per year.

President of one party with the other party controlling both Houses of Congress: Republican Presidents with a Democratic Congress produced a per year growth in GDP that averages 1.59%. Democratic Presidents with a Republican Congress produced a per year growth in GDP that averages 2.5%.

Summary of Control Data Computation with 1-Year Offset - The one-year offset produces similar results. For years Republicans controlled government policy GDP grew an average of 0.95% per year. In the 58 years Democrats controlled government policy GDP grew an average of 2.94% per year. Breaking the numbers down:

When one party controls the House, Senate and Presidency: Republicans have produced a per year growth in GDP that averages 0.22%. Democrats have produced a per year growth in GDP that averages 3.8%.

President of one party with control of one house of Congress: A Republican Presidents with Republican control of one house averaged GDP of 2.28% per year. A Democratic President with Democratic control of one house averaged GDP of 2.02%.

President of one party with the other party controlling both Houses of Congress: Republican Presidents with a Democratic Congress produced a per year growth in GDP that averaged 1.59%. Democratic Presidents with a Republican Congress produced a per year growth in GDP that averaged 2.5%.

This concludes our data summary. A much more detailed breakdown can be found in the Appendix A and spreadsheets discussed in Appendix C.

Chapter 15
Comparing GDP with High Tax Rates

The GDP figures are so completely contrary to public perceptions about who is best at managing the economy it begs further consideration.

One fact that leaps out of the Tax and GDP data is that the last 100 years can be broken down into three periods of time where the highest tax rate applied to the income of the wealthiest taxpayers remained relatively consistent. Republican low tax policies dominated in two periods. One longer period was dominated by Democratic high tax policies.

When you compare GDP during years of high tax rates on the wealthy against years with low tax rates on the wealthy it turns out the economy grew twice as fast. For this comparison we assign GDP figures to the year that taxpayers would have been planning their economic activities based on the particular tax rate. Here are the basic details:

Republican lower tax rates (top rate below 50%) have applied for 52 of the last 100 years. During that span of Republican policy control total GDP growth was 63.36%, an average growth per year of 1.2%. Here are more details on the periods when Republican policies dominated:

From 1919 to 1932 - for this period we use the tax rates applicable during 1932 on the assumption that was what people used for planning, although in 1933 both the highest income tax rate and the highest inheritance tax rate were retroactively raised to apply to transactions occurring in 1932. From 1919 to 1932 the average highest Income tax rate was 44% and the top Estate Tax rate averaged about 26%.

From 1981 to 2018 the highest income tax rate averaged around 39%, the highest inheritance tax rate averaged around 53%.

Democratic high tax policies controlled from **1932 to 1981.** The highest income tax rate went from 63% to over 90% and back down to 70%. The highest Estate tax rate was over 70%. For that forty-seven-year span GDP grew 132.78%, an average of 2.76% growth per year.

This correlations between Republican low tax policies and mediocre GDP growth and Democratic policies and more impressive GDP figures are not ironclad proof. Although it is not easy to come up with other explanations for these GDP disparities that make sense, we cannot rule out the possibility there is some other explanation. But we can cross check by ignoring party and just compare GDP against the highest tax rates on the wealthiest taxpayers.[13]

See the table of results on the next page.

---

[13] See appendix C for access to spreadsheets with a year by year breakdown

Years	# of years	Top Tax rate	GDP growth / year
1919 -1921	3	73%	-2%
1922-1923	2	58%	7.5%
1924	1	46%	1%
1925-1932*	8	25%	1%
1933-1936	4	63%	3%
1937-1940	4	79%	3.75%
1941-1943	3	81%	16.6%
1944-1963	20	91-94%	1.15%
1964-1981	18	70%	2.4%
1982-1986	5	50%	2.6%
1987	1	38.5%	3%
1988-1990	3	28%	2.3%
1991-1992	2	31%	1%
1993-2002	10	39.6%	2.2%
2003-2012	10	35%	1.88%
2013-2018	5	39.6%	1.4%

We include 1932 although after the end of the year the top tax rate was retroactively changed to 63% since taxpayers would have planned on a 25% rate.

In the 55 years where the highest tax rate exceeded 50% GDP grew by 141.7%, an average of 2.57% growth per year. In the 45 years when the highest tax rate was below 50% the total GDP growth was 78.99% for an average GDP growth of 1.75%.

If we flipped the five years the highest tax rate was right at 50% (1982 to 1986) into the high tax column the high tax years GDP growth averages 2.56% while the low tax years average GDP growth drops to 1.67%

One of the worst years for GDP, 1932, when GDP shrunk -13%, the top tax rate increase was not actually in effect during 1932. Congress applied it retroactively in early 1933 to income being reported on 1932 tax returns, so was not really a factor in taxpayer decisions in 1932.

The curious correlation between GDP and which party controls is consistent with the findings when GDP is directly compared to the high tax rates on the wealthiest taxpayers.

Another possible contributing factor to explain why GDP averages more during periods of Democratic control than during periods of Republican control could be the Federal minimum wage laws.[14] The first Federal Minimum wage law was enacted in 1938. Over the intervening 80 years Democrats have generally sought regular increases in the minimum wage, so in periods when Democratic policies were dominant there were regular minimum wage increases. The peak of purchasing power for the minimum wage was in 1968, at the end of 8 years of Democratic control of all three elective power centers.

Republicans are somewhat hostile to the idea of the minimum wage - it being government interference in the market - so when Republican policies dominate minimum wage increases are few and far between. During the decades long domination of Republican policies since 1981, the purchasing power of the minimum wage has consistently declined (see the Wikipedia article cited in the footnotes, section on Historical Trend).

---

[14] For a historical view of the minimum wage laws see the Wikipedia article on "/Minimum wage in the United States"

Another possible explanation for Democratic GDP figures trumping Republican GDP figures could be population age distribution. Economists say that how much of the population is between the age of 25 and 55, when people are at the peak of productivity, can affect how fast a growth can occur (the economic jargon is demographics).[15] As an example if only 40% of the population is in this prime productivity group growth will be lower than if 60% of the population fits in this group, since the 40% are in effect supporting 60% of the population, while the 60% load is only 40% of the population.

However, this explanation is no help to low tax advocates. The baby boomer generation caused one of the biggest bumps in history in the percentage of persons in that historical sweet spot of ages 25 to 55, and that bump was moving through the economy during the period of low tax rates from 1980 through today. On top of that women began moving into the workforce in the 1970's. That increase in the labor pool should have been an additional demographic boost on top of the boost from the large baby boomer male workforce. It is hard to avoid the suspicion the low GDP growth during the years of low maximum tax rates would have been even lower if it weren't for the benefit of more workers in prime productive years.

---

[15] For general discussion see
https://www.investopedia.com/articles/investing/012315/how-demographics-drive-economy.asp

Chapter 16
Control, Tax Rates and the National Debt

Curious Fact: The National Debt has consistently risen when Republican low tax policies control, and consistently fallen when Democratic high tax policies control.

Details - Now that we have discovered that the economy as measured by GDP has done much better under Democrats in the 100 years from 1919 to 2018, we take a look to see what happened to our National Debt during that time period. Government spending boosts GDP so the temptation for any administration is to spend money to grow the economy. Who has done the best job of managing the trade off between government expenditures and keeping debt obligations low?

Methodology - We use a ratio of debt to inflation adjusted Gross Domestic Product (GDP) as the measuring stick for where our national debt stands, rather than the absolute debt numbers. Using the ratio of debt to GDP allows us to ignore inflation in comparing debt against the income.

The Federal Government is a massive behemoth that has a lot of momentum at any given time making changing course a slow process. In attempting to compare the effects of Democratic and Republican policies on the National debt we build in a 1-year lag in computing National debt figures for each period where one party maintained control, beginning to attribute to the controlling party the figure for the year following the year they took control. For example, Republicans gained control of both houses of Congress in March of 1919, so the first National Debt number we attribute to them is for 1920. This is admittedly an arbitrary choice, in some cases perhaps the incoming party may have had a quicker impact, in some cases it may have taken longer for changes to reflect in the National Debt. But this figure will serve as an estimate that will give us an approximation of their impact on the National debt.

We begin with a summary of our findings then explain how we got there, so you can move to the next chapter at any point after the Chapter Summary and still make sense of future chapters.

Chapter Summary - Data using 1-year offset - In the last 100 years the National Debt has increased by:

61% in the 41 years Republicans controlled.

10.5% in the 59 years Democrats controlled.[16]

Discussion - We use a 1-year offset for computing National Debt on the assumption that credit or blame for debt in the year one party takes over really should be on the party giving up control. The National Debt information is derived from Internet sources:[17]

In one sense the result is no surprise. As we have seen Republicans have consistently cut taxes and backed away from taxing very high incomes at high rates. When Republicans control, they maintain a top tax rate well under 50% that applies to all taxpayers once their income reaches a relatively low level. Democrats have created more tax brackets in order to tax very high-income taxpayers' high rates once their income passes

---

[16] See Spreadsheet at the link in Appendix B.

[17] Figures for debt/GDP ratio - since 1929 taken from
https://www.thebalance.com/national-debt-by-year-compared-to-gdp-and-major-events-3306287
Pre 1929 debt/GDP in part derived from
https://www.usgovernmentdebt.us/spending_chart_1918_1930USp_1 9s2li011tcn_H0f_Accumulated_Gross_Federal_Debt

some threshold far beyond the income of most Americans. As a quick review -

When Republicans dominated government from 1919 through 1932 the top rate of tax fell from 73% to 25% over a fourteen-year span.

When Democrats dominated government from 1933 through 1980, they increased the number of tax brackets and the average top tax rate was about 85%.

Republicans have dominated tax policy from 1981 to the present and have drastically reduced brackets and the average top rate has been below 40%.

The Democrats have been vastly more fiscally responsible despite the fact the biggest yearly jumps in the National debt happened during the periods of attributed to Democratic control. In 1919 the national debt jumped 17% in the aftermath of World War I (in the Democrats column due to the one-year offset). Then during World War II when Democrats controlled the debt rose at an average of 11.5% of GDP per year from 1942 to 1947.

The National Debt and Control Scorecard -

Republicans controlled all branches of elective government for 21 years during which the National Debt increased a net 19% of GDP.

Democrats controlled all branches of elective government for 31 years during which the National Debt increased a net 4.95%.

When Congress was split with a Republican President (8 years) the National Debt increased a net 39% of GDP. With a Democratic President (5 years) the National Debt increased a net 15% of GDP.

When one party controlled Congress but not the Presidency (34 years) with a Republican President and Democratic Congress (20 years) the National debt did not increase or decrease. With a Democratic President and Republican Congress (12 years) the debt increased a net of 3% of GDP.

As noted above totaling up all the periods when one party controlled 2 of the 3 elective power centers, we find that Republicans controlled 42 years with a net increase in the National Debt of 63% while Democrats controlled 59 years with a net increase in the National Debt of 10.5%.[18]

However, a simpler and perhaps more telling comparison is to look at the three broad periods where one party dominated policy.

When Republicans dominated from 1919 to 1933 the National debt at first went down for slightly but by 1933 as the Democrats took over it was 4.5% higher than it had been at the end of World War I when the Republicans took over.

From 1933 through 1981, although Republicans controlled Congress twice for two years, and in 1954-1955 with a Republican President, the policies instituted by Franklin Roosevelt in the 1930's were not substantially altered. In 1933, in the depths of the depression the National Debt amounted to 39% of GDP. Despite funding World War II, the Korean War, putting a man on the moon, and fighting the Vietnam war, in 1981 the Democrats handed Ronald Reagan a lower National debt than what existed when they took over in 1933 - a net reduction over those 38 years from 39% down to 31%.

Since 1981 Republican low tax policies pushed through by Ronald Reagan have dominated Government. Although Democrats twice had two years controlling Congress with Democratic Presidents, and had a couple years with a Democratic President and

---

[18] The two totals add up to odd years due to the one-year offset.

Senate, no change was made in the basic Reagan formula of low tax rates and lots of defense spending.

The 1981 debt of 31% of GDP has now increased to the point we owe over 100% of GDP and the percentage is rising quickly following the Trump Tax cuts.

Republicans have historically characterized Democrats as fiscally irresponsible. Yet over the last 100 years, when Democratic policies dominated between 1933 and 1980, we as a country managed to fund World War II, the Korean War and the Vietnam war, Social Security, unemployment programs and Medicare, and put a man on the moon, while reducing the National Debt from 39% of GDP to 34% of GDP. In contrast since 1981 Republican low tax policies have increased the National Debt from 31% of GDP to over 100% of GDP.

Chapter 17
Comparing Control to United States Net Worth

As individuals when we figure out whether we are accumulating wealth or losing wealth we offset increases in income with increases in debt. If we use that same process to compare how the United States has done over the last 100 years during periods of Republican control and periods of Democratic control the difference is astonishing.

We have already seen that GDP has grown far faster during periods of Democratic policy dominance than it has during periods of Republican dominance.

We have also seen that the National debt has grown far faster under Republican policy dominance than under Democratic policy dominance.

Suppose we take the GDP figures and subtract the increase in National debt?

The Killer Curious Fact:

In the 42 years Republicans had majority control of government net GDP growth was 35%. In the same period the net increase in the National debt was 61% of GDP. If we subtract the net increase in the National debt from the net GDP growth, we end up with a net loss of -26% of GDP, an average loss of -.5% of GDP per year of Republican Control.

In the 58 years Democrats had majority control of government net GDP growth was 170% and the net increase in the National debt was 10%. Subtracting the National Debt increase from the GDP increase we find a net GDP gain of 160%, an average net GDP gain of 2.75% per year.

So, on average the net worth of the United States per year under Democrats over 58 years increased by 3.25% per year more than the net worth per year in the 42 years of Republican control.

Chapter 18
Control and Business Formation

Republicans have always touted themselves as the party of business (and by implication wealth for everybody). We have seen that when their policies control GDP is lower, and the National Debt higher. But perhaps somehow their policies still increase the total number of businesses?

There doesn't seem to be a lot of data on the number of businesses historically created or existing as one goes back in time. But there is some data for the last 40 to 50 years. Republican ideology gained the upper hand in 1981 with the election of Ronald Reagan and then doubled down when the Republicans took control of Congress in 1995 and held it for 12 years. Can find some data to suggest that their policies facilitated the start of lots of new businesses?

The data doesn't work out that way.

According to the small business council 98% of the workers in the United States work in small business with less than 20 employees.[19] Small business accounted for over 60% of new jobs between 1993 and 2016. A curiously revealing result comes from the web site statista.com[20] which looks at small business that employs people, and small businesses that do not employ people. In 1997 after the Republican Congress had made major changes to the countries tax and regulatory scheme rooted in the notion of unleashing

---
[19] https://sbecouncil.org/about-us/facts-and-data/
[20] https://www.statista.com/statistics/257521/number-of-small-businesses-in-the-us/

business, about 5.5 million small businesses existed that employed people. In 2016 the number was 5.6 million. A net gain of less 2% despite the fact the countries population grew about 12%, from 272 million to 323 Million during that two-decade span.

A CNN money article from 2106 surveyed available data and found new business creation in the U.S. was at nearly a 40-year low. Only 452,835 firms were born in 2014, according to the most recent U.S. Census data released before the article, well below the 500,000 to 600,000 new companies that were started in the U.S. every year from the late 1970s to the mid-2000s.[21]

Even the number of public companies traded on stock markets has shrunk. Bloomberg[22] says: *"...the universe of such companies has been shrinking in the U.S. New businesses have been offering shares to the public at less than half the rate of the 1980s and 1990s. Mergers and acquisitions have eliminated hundreds more. About 3,600 firms were listed on U.S. stock exchanges at the end of 2017, down more than half from 1997."*

This Bloomberg opinion piece argues it is not necessarily a bad thing - it notes the still existing public companies have become ever bigger, and there seems to be no shortage of capital. But given the correlation with reduced GDP and increased public debt that occurred during that period it clearly was not a good thing, and raises the suggestion fewer businesses meant fewer people doing well economically. Which raises the question of income inequality.

---

[21] https://money.cnn.com/2016/09/08/news/economy/us-startups-near-40-year-low/index.html
[22] https://www.bloomberg.com/opinion/articles/2018-04-09/where-have-all-the-u-s-public-companies-gone

Chapter 19
Control and Income inequality

Curious Fact: In the last 100 years when Republicans have controlled policy the rich get richer and the poor get poorer. When Democrats have controlled policy the rich still get richer but the poor also do much better.

Data Summary: When Republicans controlled policy from 1919 to 1932 the share of the total US wealth owned by the 1% of the wealthiest taxpayers in 1919 was 35% of the national wealth. By 1932 they owned 40% for a net increase of 5% of the wealth.

When Democrats controlled policy from 1933 to 1980 the share of the 1% shrank from 40% to 24% for a net decrease of 16%.

Since Republicans took control of policy in 1981 the 1%'s share of the wealth has grown from 24% to the current 37% for a net increase of 13%

Details - Income inequality measures how much rich folks make compared to how much regular folks make.

Republicans often characterize any mention of income inequality as "class warfare". Curiously, as the correlations in this volume demonstrate, Republicans have no problem whatsoever making the law work to the best advantage of the wealthy, it becomes class warfare when the not so wealthy try to shape policy to their advantage.

Income inequality data, unlike tax, GDP or National debt data, is not widely available in publicly available sources, so our cited sources are often to more obscure academic publications.

This topic has been so heavily politicized that one might assume a more equal America is something only Democratic voters would like. But a 2011 survey of thousands of Americans across the political, geographical, socio-economic and gender spectrum found all assumed America was more equal than it actually is.[23]

When asked how much wealth (property and stocks - debt) was held by the top 20% most people assumed that the top 20% had about 59% of the wealth.

The real number was 84% of the wealth, while the poorest 124.6 million Americans had negative wealth, more debt than assets.

Across all demographics, nearly everyone agreed that this was not ideal. When asked to design their ideal society, participants gave the top fifth of earners about 32% of the wealth. This was remarkably consistent across demographics, so that even top earning Republicans did not want a society where the richest fifth had more than 40% of the wealth.

But even the richest fifth of the country are poor compared to the top 1% of earners. In 2016 the top 1% of the population had 38.6% of the wealth. 3.2 million Americans had all the wealth that the most conservative demographic would distribute to 64.7 million Americans.

With this in mind, we look to see if there are correlations between who controls policy and income inequality.

For this computation we again employ a one-year lag to account for the time it takes a new Congress and/or Administration to get up and running.

---

[23] http://www.people.hbs.edu/mnorton/norton%20ariely%20in%20press.pdf

Year-by-year Details
1919-1932 - Republicans Control

Calvin Coolidge, President from 1923-28, summed up his view of government stating "It is much more important to kill bad bills than to pass good ones." This period followed the classic boom and bust cycle that characterized Republican periods of policy control. A boom from 1922 to 1929 saw real wages in manufacturing go up by 1.4 percent a year, paltry compared to the value of stocks that rose 16.4 percent a year.[24]

The speculative stock market bubble ended in the 1929 Stock Market Crash. Thousands of banks failed resulting in hundreds of thousands of depositors losing their savings. The real estate market collapsed. Homes were being foreclosed at a rate that, in 1933, exceeded 1000 new foreclosures every day[25] despite the fact the property was often worth only a fraction of the value of the loan. Farmers were hit hardest. Between 1929 and 1933, fully a third of all Americans lost their farms.[26] Because property is usually the largest asset of a person's wealth, this meant independent farmer and middle-class wealth was collapsing. The people who had less to lose often lost it all.

The country as a whole had GDP in 1920 of 88.4 billion. By 1933 GDP had dropped to 57.2 Billion, a net loss of productive activity of over $30 billion. In 1920, the 1% had 35.64% of the wealth. By 1933, they had 40.27% of the remaining wealth.

---

[24] P. 373
http://library.uniteddiversity.coop/More_Books_and_Reports/Howard_Zinn-A_peoples_history_of_the_United_States.pdf

[25] https://www.encyclopedia.com/education/news-and-education-magazines/housing-1929-1941

[26]
http://www.montgomeryschoolsmd.org/uploadedFiles/schools/northbethesdams/mediacenter/projects/grade8/farmforeclosure.pdf

1933-1946 - Democratic Control

Democratic control led to a reversal in Government policy. Roosevelt Democrats embraced a New Deal Policy of constant and ambitious government action. The reversal produced hyperbolic comments from some ideologically leaning right. The English Author H.G. Wells said, *"The New Deal is plainly an attempt to achieve a working socialism and avert a social collapse in America; it is extraordinarily parallel to the successive 'policies' and 'plans' of the Russian experiment. Americans shirk the word 'socialism', but what else can one call it?"* [27]

Former president Herbert Hoover (in office when the Stock Market crash occurred), said, *"The New Deal repudiation of democracy has left the Republican Party alone the guardian of the Ark of the Covenant with its charter of freedom."*[28] (Maybe the most massively mixed metaphor in history?).

The actual results of the policy swing - In 1934, the 1% had 40.92% of American wealth. By 1947, the 1% share had shrunk to 28.63% of the wealth, even as inflation adjusted national GDP increased nearly 250%. With this economic growth, even the 1% did better than they did in the 20s. And everyone else did much, much better.

1947 to 1980 - Democratic Control

Overview - For the 33 years following the end of World War II the policies of Roosevelt - high progressive taxation and active state enterprise such as the Dwight D. Eisenhower federal highway system, produced a consistently falling National debt along with strong GDP

---

[27] https://www.voltairenet.org/IMG/pdf/Wells_New_World_Order-3.pdf
[28] http://www.austincc.edu/lpatrick/his2341/The%20Challenge%20to%20Liberty.html

growth. In 1947 the top 1% of taxpayers owned 28% of the wealth. By 1980 that share had declined to 23.8%.

Details:

1947 to 1948 - With a Republican Congress and Democratic President the share of the 1% decreased from 28.02% to 27.14%.

1949 to 1952 - With a Democratic Congress and President the share of the 1% continued to decrease, from 28.48% in 1950 to 26.49% in 1953.

1953 to 1954 - With a Republican Congress and President the wealth share of the 1% increases very slightly from 27.18% to 27.48%.

1955 to 1980 - With Democrats controlling Congress and alternating Republican (14 years total) and Democratic (12 years total) administrations the wealth share of the 1% steadily decreased from 27.84% in 1956 to 23.80% by 1981. It is important to keep in mind it wasn't that the rich were getting poorer, quite the contrary. The rich were still getting richer, but so was everyone else. But policy reversed with Ronald Reagan's election in 1980.

1981 to 1986 - Republican Control

Ronald Reagan combined with a Republican Senate and a compliant Democratic House to reshape Government policy. James Baker, who was White House Chief of Staff from 1981-85, and then Secretary of the Treasury for the rest of the Reagan years, rephrasing the words of Calvin Coolidge back in the 1920's, summed up the new federal philosophy when he said "sometimes an active policy is best advanced by doing

---

[29] https://www.linkedin.com/pulse/words-wisdom-james-baker-iii-william-bill-simpson-obe

nothing until the right time - or never."[29] The highest tax rate was cut to below 40% and has stayed below 40% since. As the National debt began to grow rapidly wealth distribution reverses to flow back up. The 1% went from having 23.73% of wealth in 1982, to 24.61% in 1987.

1987 to 1994, following the pattern established in the new "Reagan" economic era with low taxes and high debt, the wealthiest share grew again from 26.57% to 27.92%.

1995 to 2008 - The 1% share of the wealth increased from 28.58% to 36.15%.

From 1995 through 2000 the Republican Congress pushed tax cuts on Capital gains and stock dividends, made speculating in Real Estate more tax advantaged, sparking a bubble in housing and stocks.

From 2001 through 2006 the Republican Congress and President (GW Bush) cut the top tax rate even as we go to war in Iraq. The National debt jumps up. The Housing market bubble peaks in 2006 then begins the slow-motion collapse that leads to the Great recession.

In 2007 and 2008 the Republican President (Bush) and Senate and Democratic House struggled to put a lid on the economic collapse we now call the Great Recession. The top tax rate stays below 40%. The slow housing market collapse continues until the fall of 2008 when big investment banks collapse and President Bush begins the bail out big investment banks to avoid complete financial panic.

2009 to 2014 - The share of the 1% decreased from 37.57% to 37.24% in 2014. In 2009 and 2010 the Democratic President (Obama) and Congress walk in the door as the world economy is threatening to collapse. The bailouts are completed, Obamacare enacted, as the top tax rate remains 38%. The national debt continues its relentless rise.

2011 to 2014 - The Democratic President (Obama) and Senate can do little with the Republican House that does not believe in compromise, although the top tax rate goes up to 39%, a change accomplished during the prior period of Democratic control of all three elective branches. The National debt continues to rise.

Since 2015 income inequality has resumed its rise.[30]

How Economists View Income Inequality

This focus on the wealth of the 1% may seem unrepresentative. But the mathematical tool that professional economists use to measure income inequality, the Gini Coefficient tells the same story. A Gini Coefficient score of 1 would indicate the wealthy controlled everything; a score of 0 would be a perfectly equal society.

In 1918 the Gini Score of the US was .41. That number increased under Republican policies to .49 in 1929, fell back to .37 by the end of WWII in 1945, where it remained until the late 1970's. The Gini Coefficient of the US has consistently risen since to about .45, considerably worse than other comparable countries.[31] The average GINI Coefficient of OECD (nations in the developed world) is .32.

---

[30] https://www.cnbc.com/2018/07/19/income-inequality-continues-to-grow-in-the-united-states.html
[31] All of these numbers are from this database, as are the other numbers cited in this chapter.
https://www.chartbookofeconomicinequality.com/inequality-by-country/usa/

Chapter 20
Infrastructure

Although not directly related to the thrust of this volume it is worth mentioning that the surprising GDP correlation of low growth during Republican periods of control could also be partly related to a factor not directly addressed in the earlier chapters.

When running the show Republicans do not fund infrastructure. Although data from 100 years ago is sparse, since World War II the nation has regularly invested more in infrastructure during periods of Democratic control, and less on infrastructure during periods of Republican control.

Even Republican President Dwight D. Eisenhower's pet project, the Interstate Highway System, an expansion on a proposal of Franklin D. Roosevelts in 1939, was not enacted during the two years Eisenhower had a Republican majority in Congress. It was introduced and passed in the two years after the Democrats took majority control of both houses of Congress

Republicans have dominated the since 1980 so we all now spend more time sitting stuck in traffic, or in long lines at airports, limiting what we can accomplish in a day.

Section D - Indirect Impacts

Chapter 21 - Control and Health Care
Chapter 22 - Control and the Housing Market
Chapter 23 - Control and Asset Bubbles
Chapter 24 - Control and Personal Capital
Chapter 25 - Control and the Stock Market
Chapter 26 - Vocation of the Presidents
Chapter 27 - Control and CEO Pay

Chapter 21
Control and Health Care

Curious Facts:

As a country we spend about 16% of GDP a year on Healthcare, our total expenditures are 40% more than any other country in the world, yet the people of many countries enjoy better care, live longer and their infant mortality rates are lower.[32] Despite pouring money into healthcare compared to the other 10 most developed Western democracies we rank at the bottom in health care effectiveness.

The basic difference is every other country has some form of Universal Health Care. When Republicans have been in control, improving health care has seldom been an issue on their agenda and they have often actively opposed healthcare reform. When Democrats have been in control, they have sought to enact Universal Health care since the 1930's but were unable to get health care reform enacted until Obamacare.

Health Care Overview

Our neighbor, Canada only spends about 60% as much as we do per person.[33] Studies have found Canadians have a higher life expectancy and lower mortality. Government accounts for about 70% of Canadian health care spending.

England, our cultural home in many ways, has a single-payer system where Government runs healthcare - socialized medicine. The quality of outcomes is comparable between the US and England but England

---

[32] https://en.wikipedia.org/wiki/Health_care_prices_in_the_United_States
[33] https://en.wikipedia.org/wiki/Comparison_of_the_healthcare_systems_in_Canada_and_the_United_States

spends about 8.4% of GDP on Healthcare - around half of what Health Care costs us.

Since the Ronald Reagan era re-established the pre-Great Depression Republican notion that business does everything better than government Republicans have largely opposed Government involvement in Health Care and stymied efforts to enact Universal Health.

A Really Curious Fact

Perhaps the oldest socialized medicine system in the World was created by the United States government after the Civil War and still exists today. The Veterans Administration (VA) Hospital system owns their own Hospitals, hire their own Doctors, and conducts their own research. It is a Government funded and run program from the ground up. The Veterans Administration Hospitals are the largest single hospital system in the United States.

No doubt the first thing that comes to mind about the VA Hospital system is the frequent scandals arising from bad management or neglect by the (often) political hacks appointed by each administration to run the system.

However, a Fortune magazine article (May 11, 2006) found the VA provides some of the best quality care in the United States at a cost of about 80% of the cost per patient of the countries private systems. A Rand study from April 2018 confirmed that the quality of care at VA Hospitals was as good as private hospitals.

Our "free market" medical care system is about 20% more expensive than our own government bureaucracy run by political hacks that still manages to provide quality care.

Why Doesn't the Free Market Work for Healthcare?

A free market works efficiently only if buyers are not acting under compulsion. When we go out to buy a car, if it is too expensive, we just walk away, or go buy a used car, or a bike, or take a bus. When enough of us just walk away the industry has to find a way to lower costs to survive.

We generally don't have the option of walking away from healthcare. If we have a child with cancer, we can't just walk away until the price comes down. In the purchase of medical services (by dollars spent - healthy people don't use much health care - sick people use almost all of it) most of the buyers are acting under compulsion - the threat of serious debilitation or death. A key market force that controls costs is missing in a private medical marketplace.

For a historical overview of health care in the United States see Appendix D.

Chapter 22
Control and Housing Market

Overall, the last 100 years has been a very good time for most American agents and people wanting to buy homes. The proportion of the population living in a house they owned went from 46% in 1900[34] to 66% in 2000[35].

Most of this growth occurred in the twenty-year period from 1940-1960, when the homeownership rate exploded from 44% to 62%. However, the growth has not been steady as policy see-sawed. Republicans have consistently pushed government out of involvement in the market, while Democrats have consistently sought to use government to address weaknesses in the market.

Curious Fact:

In the last 100 years home ownership has grown during periods of Democratic policy dominance and shrunk during periods of Republican policy dominance.

During periods of Republican control more people lose their homes to foreclosure, while there are fewer foreclosures during periods of Democratic control.

For a more detailed historical overview of homeownership and housing policy see Appendix E.

---

[34] https://dqydj.com/historical-homeownership-rate-in-the-united-states-1890-present/

[35] https://www.census.gov/hhes/www/housing/census/historic/ownershipbyrace.html

Chapter 23
Control and Asset Bubbles

Curious Fact:

Asset bubbles or suspected asset bubbles happen regularly when Republican policies dominate, but are almost unheard of when Democratic policies have dominated.

Details:

There are many possible investments that are not risk-taking enterprises - assets where the value is inherent in the asset rather than being created by producing something or providing some service. Examples are gold or other precious metals, real estate, art, antiques or any other item that can be held then sold at some future date.

People can also invest in existing stocks or bonds where the price is based on known facts about the underlying businesses so risk of catastrophic loss is low.

Most assets have a predictable value when supply and demand are in sync. The value of an asset should track inflation absent improvements to the asset or supply and demand anomalies. Sometimes, however, people become convinced a particular asset or asset class is going to increase in value far in excess of what the traditional valuation would suggest. The asset becomes infected by a speculative fever. Economists call them asset bubbles - like a bubble they expand rapidly then burst.

There are so many potential assets a detailed look at asset bubbles in the last 100 years would be really difficult. So instead we turn to the Internet. We start with an article titled "Five of the Largest Asset Bubbles in History" from the investment web page Investopedia.[36]

The first two cited are historical events from which the whole concept of an asset bubble was developed.

First was the 1630's financial mania for tulips in Holland. From 1630 to 1631 the price of Tulips exploded. At one point some tulips were valued more than a luxury home. Then the priced collapsed.

Number 2 on the list was the South Sea bubble. In 1720 the British Government promised the South Sea Company in England a virtual monopoly on trade with Spain's South American colonies. Tales of wild riches caused shares in the company to surge in price nearly 1000% in 6 months, then the prices collapsed causing a severe economic downturn.

The third on the Investopedia list is the Japan Stock and Housing Market Bubble from 1986 to 1991. The bubble was triggered by the Japanese Government overreacting to a recession by dropping interest rates, setting of a speculative bubble in stocks and housing that collapsed in 1991 and sent Japan into decades of stagnant economic conditions.

The last two bubbles on the list both happened after Republicans took over Congress in 1995.

First the Dot-Com stock market bubble that collapsed in 2001 and sent the value of tech stocks into an 80% drop in value, triggering a recession. Then a speculative bubble in house prices in the early 2000's followed by a price collapse between 2006 and 2009 was the major component in the Great Recession.

---

[36] https://www.investopedia.com/articles/personal-finance/062315/five-largest-asset-bubbles-history.asp

A Wikipedia[37] article on asset bubbles lists other bubbles that occurred in the United States. In the last 100 years these include a Florida speculative land bubble in the early 1920's, the Roaring Twenties stock market bubble that crashed in 1929, a gold and silver bubble from 1976 to 1980 sparked by high inflation and various commodity bubbles in the 2000's.

Of the five listed bubbles in the United States in these two lists four occurred during periods when Republicans controlled policy. The only bubble that occurred during the period of Democratic control was a bubble specific to big investors trying to corner the market in certain precious metals and did not affect normal folk much

---

[37] https://en.wikipedia.org/wiki/Economic_bubble#Examples_of_asset_bubbles

Chapter 24
Control and Personal Capital

Curious Fact:

When Republicans control policy higher education becomes impossibly expensive for many people. When Democratic policies control education is more widely affordable across the economic spectrum.

Details:

When economists speak of investment capital, they include personal capital. Historically personal capital, the skills we develop individually that allow us to create wealth, is difficult to measure. Personal capital can be developed in many ways, even as a circumstantial combination of your parents and surroundings as you grow up with your personal inclinations and talents. Data is sparse on how people have done in developing personal capital in the last 100 years.

Education does give some insight into how supportive Republicans and Democrats have been toward encouraging personal capital.

Even 100 years ago virtually all Americans had access tax supported public education through high school, still the case today. In 1920 the ability to read and write was all the qualification needed for many good jobs in manufacturing. Today one needs far more developed skills for any job not at the bottom of the economic ladder. But the need for and access to higher education has changed dramatically.

We resort again to the Internet for data. According to the Competitive Enterprise Institute[38] since

---

[38] https://cei.org/blog/mind-boggling-increase-tuition-1960-even-

1960 law school tuition has increased 1000% after adjusting for inflation. This author's personal experience suggests the change between 1960 and 1980 was not dramatic. In 1978-79, this authors third year at University of California Davis law school tuition was $723.50. Today tuition is $49,455 per year.

The Competitive Enterprise Institute also notes as of 2015 the cost of college tuition has doubled the rate of inflation since 1980. According to wikipedia[39] state support for college education has fallen 26% since the 1980's. In 2011 for the first time in US history public State Colleges and Universities took in more money from tuition than from state support.

Democrats broadly supported higher Education in the years their policies dominated from 1934 to 1980.

Since 1980 as Republican tax and small government policies came to dominate, state support for higher education has dropped as tuition exploded. Students have had to turn to more expensive private sector loans and private colleges that sometimes just go out of business if they aren't making enough money - leaving students with nothing but the debt they incurred.

Republicans pay lip service to the development of personal capital being vital to growing our economy but they have consistently made it more difficult for those without family wealth to gain an education.

Chapter 25

---

students-learn-less-and-less

[39]

https://en.wikipedia.org/wiki/College_tuition_in_the_United_States#History

Control and the Stock Market

A Particularly Curious Fact:

If there were one part of the economy one would expect historically would prosper under Republicans it would be the Stock Market.

But over the last 100 years markets have prospered under Democratic Administrations averaging over 6% per year returns while during Republican Administrations the market has averaged a net loss of about -1% per year.

Details:

For this chapter, given the wealth of data relating to Stock Markets, we again depart from our usual format and turn instead to the generally Republican leaning business press, although the articles tend to focus on the party of the President and pay less attention to the balance of power within Congress.

We begin with a study by Barclays Capital reported in the Economist Magazine issue of October 6, 2012 (p.84) that found between 1929 and 2011 the average price change on stocks, adjusted for inflation, during the 40 years we have had Republican President's was slightly less than zero per year. The 44 years where we have had Democratic Presidents, on the other hand, averaged about 7% increase per year.

The study found even if you look only at the years where a Republican President's party controlled both houses of Congress, the real average return on stocks is negative. Predictably, given that bonds do well when investor's retreat from equities, bond prices when we had Republican President's averaged a gain in bond values of 1.9% while Democrats saw a loss of just under 1%.

The study found the inflation rate has been slightly higher under Democratic Presidents than Republican Presidents (3.5% to 3%), but far from enough to explain away the Republicans poor record.

The advantage to Democratic Presidents goes beyond prices to income. The article cites calculations[40] that the top 20% of earners, between 1952 and 2004, did better under Democratic Presidents than Republican Presidents (1.37% to 0.92%). So did the poor (bottom 20%) who gained 1.56% a year under Democrats, and lost 0.32% under Republicans.

As our prior chapters have demonstrated, the article notes a big part of the Republicans problem is that they just seem to be running the show when calamitous collapses in stock prices occur. In 1929 Herbert Hoover was President, in 1973-74 it was Richard Nixon, in 1987 Ronald Reagan and in 2001 and again in 2008 it was George Bush. The stock market seldom crashes when a Democrat is President. Roosevelt in 1935-36 is the only one even beginning to rise to the level of the classic Republican collapses.[41]

Business publications have been aware of this particular Curious Correlation for some time. They generally spend a lot of time explaining how it's not that Democrats are better on policy - Republicans are just unlucky.

A January 22, 2004 article in CNN Money, "*Surprise: Dems are better for rallies*" by CNN Staff Writer Alexandra Twin cites a study from UCLA that looked at the stock market from 1927 to 1999 that found the market rose an average of 11% per year under Democrats and sunk an average of -2% per year under

---

[40] "From Unequal Democracy: The Political Economy of the New Gilded Age" (Larry Bartels)
[41] See also US News and World Report - Money article of November 5, 2012, "*Which Party Does the Market Perform Best Under*" by staff writer Chris Gay.

Republicans. The study concluded the Stock Market performs better and is less volatile under Democrats.

In an article in Forbes Magazine for July 26, 2016[42] notes that performance under Democratic Presidents has been much better but argues that one can't conclude the reason was because Democrats held the Presidency since there is no conclusive evidence that the President impacts Stock prices.

Similar sentiments are found in an article in the Business Insider of December 20, 2015[43] although it states at one point *"There really shouldn't be any debate; on a historical basis, Democratic presidents are better for the stock market. The saying that Republican Presidents are better than Democrats for investors continues to be one of the bigger misconceptions there is in the investment world."*

The data in this volume suggests this misconception pales in comparison to the misconception that Republicans are better at managing the economy.

---

[42] *"Democrats vs. Republicans: Who Is Better for The Stock Market?"* by Peter Lazeroff

[43] *The stock market loves Democratic presidents more than Republicans"* by Myles Udland.

Chapter 26
President's Party Affiliation and Vocation

A Curious Introductory Fact:

In the last 100 years five Presidents, all Republicans, came to the Presidency riding reputations from business careers. How did they do in Politics?

Warren G. Harding (1921-1923 - died in office) was the first President to have a cabinet member jailed for accepting bribes. Harding initiated the Republican policy choices that led us into the Great Depression.

Herbert Hoover (1929-1933) saw GDP shrink an average of about 10% per year in his four years as the National debt expanded.

George H. Bush (1989-1993) saw GDP growth average .48% per year during his 4 years, significantly trailing growth in the National debt.

George Walker Bush (2001-2009) left office as the country plunged into the depths of the Great Recession.

President Trump was the fifth. Numerous members of the Trump administration have already been convicted of crimes and in the first three years of his administration growth in the National debt exceeded GDP growth. Once Covid-19 arrived the debt exploded as the economy contracted.

Presidents of the Last 100 Years

Why does the "misconception" that Republicans are better for the Stock Market noted in the prior chapter exist? Consider the vocation of Presidents.

Between 1919 and 2018 eighteen different people (men actually but let's not make it a gender thing) have been President. Five Republican Presidents came out of a significant business career and no Democrats. The two Presidents who were at the helm when we slid into the Great Depression and Great Recession were both businessmen (Hoover and GW Bush).

This seems to suggest business folk are not necessarily very good at managing an economy. It is not difficult to conjecture why that might be.

Ask yourself for a two-word description of the goal of business. Pretty easy, right? "Make money". Now ask yourself for a two-word description for a goal of politics. Not so easy. Easier if your only concern is "getting elected", but enormously difficult if you actually want to be successful at the job. What do you focus on as your goal? Making everybody happy?

History suggests business folk think solving the relatively straightforward problem of how to turn a profit qualifies them as experts to try to solve the enormously complex moving target that is good policy for the country. Being a good politician isn't about following a logical path to a clear goal. It is about balancing competing and sometimes incompatible goals.

In business often an easy answer to improving your balance sheet is to cut expenses by firing people. When a company fires a bunch of people, the business is more profitable and the fired folks are no longer the businesses problem.

But the more businesses fire people the bigger the problem for government. A President can't fire voters to make budget problems go away, but Presidents from a business background seem to have a hard time grasping this reality.

In foreign relations the focus on balance sheets that Presidents who come out of a business background exhibit causes them to misjudge the motives of other world leaders. They negotiate based on how they perceive relative strength, raising the stakes when they have a good hand thinking other countries will fold when they realize they have a bad hand. But other countries politicians often operate on a different logic - they are about their own political survival. So heavy handed tactics towards another country get turned by that countries politicians into a tool to prop up their own popularity by standing up to the bully.

Tariffs are a good example of how business thinking seldom produces a result that improves the countries overall wealth. Tariffs seeking to shelter US business from foreign competition are good for some business owners, and good for some labor in the short run. But it is bad for consumption as it makes goods more expensive so in the end consumers end up buying less.

Tariffs are also bad for innovation as stress often fosters innovation, while tariffs allow business to sit back and continue doing what they have been doing instead of finding new and better ways to do things. Think big clunky cars with tail fins in the late 1950's that led to a wave of fuel-efficient and reliable foreign makes moving into the US market in the 1960's.

Details on Presidents from 1919 to 2018.

There have been eight Democratic Presidents.

Woodrow Wilson, FDR, Harry Truman, John Kennedy, Lyndon Johnson, Jimmy Carter, Bill Clinton and Barack Obama.

No Democratic President ever came out of a significant experience in the business world (although some had business interests from wealthy families). Two came out of academics (Wilson and Johnson). Three were lawyers who went straight into politics after law school (Roosevelt, Clinton and Obama). Three came out of military early in life and went into politics (Truman, Kennedy and Carter).

Of the 10 Republican Presidents five came out of careers in the business (Hoover, Harding, GH Bush, GW Bush and Trump). Two came to politics out of military careers (Eisenhower and Ford). Two were lawyers who went straight into politics (Coolidge and Nixon). Ronald Reagan was an entertainer and motivational speaker.

We list all 18 Presidents in the last 100 years with their pre-political vocations.[44]

1919-1920 - Democrat Woodrow Wilson was a President of Princeton University before moving into politics.

1921 to 1923 - Republican Warren G. Harding was a newspaper owner who used the newspaper to help him launch a political career.

1923 to 1929 - Republican Calvin Coolidge was a lawyer who turned quickly to politics.

1929 to 1933 - Republican Herbert Hoover was a mining engineer and businessman who moved into government during World War I.

1933 to 1945 - Democrat Franklin D. Roosevelt was a lawyer who went straight into politics.

1945 to 1953 - Democrat Harry Truman briefly owned a clothing store after mustering out of the Army after World War I but moved quickly into politics.

1953-1961 - Republican Dwight D. Eisenhower was a career military officer.

---

[44] Information on all Presidents from their Wikipedia biography

1961-1963 - Democrat John Kennedy moved from military service into politics.

1963-1969 - Democrat Lyndon Johnson was a high school teacher before politics.

1969-1974 - Republican Richard Nixon practiced law before moving into politics.

1974-1977 - Republican Gerald Ford moved from military service in World War II into politics.

1977-1981 - Democrat Jimmy Carter was born into a wealthy family of peanut farmers but after a seven-year career as a Naval Officer he moved into politics.

1981-1989 - Republican Ronald Reagan was an actor then motivational speaker before a late in life move into politics.

1989-1993 - Republican George H. Bush was born to a wealthy New England family and built a Texas oil business after World War II, then moved into politics.

1993-2001 - Democrat Bill Clinton was a lawyer who went directly into politics.

2001-2009 - Republican George W. Bush was in the oil business then an owner of the Texas Rangers baseball team before moving into politics.

2009-2017 - Democrat Barack Obama was a lawyer who moved directly into politics.

2017-? - Republican Donald Trump was born into a wealthy New York family who move into the family business as a real estate investor/promoter, then became an entertainer before moving into politics.

Chapter 27
Control and CEO Pay

Curious Fact:

In the last nearly 40 years since Republican policies began dominating public policy CEO Pay has risen 935%, while worker pay has increased 11%. CEO pay in that period has grown 70% faster than the value of the Corporations CEO's run.

Details:

When corporations were developing back in the 18th century the CEO and other corporate officers were simply employees whose compensation was monitored by a board of directors and the investors who ultimately controlled the corporation. That is no longer the case.

Today huge companies with tens or hundreds of thousands of shareholders dominate the economy. Most shareholders are not involved, nor interested in getting involved, nor would they have the ability to participate meaningfully in managing the corporation. Corporate directors and officers' effectively control most big modern corporations.

Data for CEO pay is sparse as you go back in time so we cannot do a strict control comparison, but it is clear that since Republican policies took over in the early 1980's CEO pay has gone on an unprecedented rise.

From the Great Depression until the late 1970's CEO compensation declined in World War II before experiencing a modest steady increase into the 1970's. Since 1978 the paycheck CEO's take home has risen 90 times faster than the paycheck of the average worker.[45]

The average workers pay has risen 11% while CEO pay has risen 935%.[46] CEO pay has increased 70% faster than the value of the underlying companies the CEO's are running.

---

[45] "The CEO Pay Machine" by Steven Clifford, a former CEO. Although this topic will only be touched on briefly in this volume, this book is a witty, well written and astonishing in detailing the complex way corporate officers have conspired to take a bigger and bigger chunk of the wealth generated by corporations. Blue rider press/Penguin Random House LLC, 2017,
[46] https://www.cnbc.com/2018/01/22/heres-how-much-ceo-pay-has-increased-compared-to-yours-over-the-years.html

Section E -

Summary - Making Sense of the Data

Chapter 28 - Summary of these Curious Correlations
Chapter 29 -Understanding these Curious Correlations
Chapter 30 - It's Not About the People

Chapter 28
Summary of these Curious Correlations

As we have seen in the prior Chapters the conventional wisdom that Republicans are better at managing the economy stands the data on its head. In the last 100 years the United States has grown far faster, incurred less debt, the housing market has been more stable, wealth has been more broadly spread across society - even the Stock Market has done better when Democrats set the basic policies.

Republicans, when in control of the Federal agenda have regularly and predictably produced slower growth and large increases in the National Debt, presided over booms and busts in the housing market and played a big part in pushing the country into the most expensive and inefficient health care system in the world. Not to mention income inequality that advances when Republican policies run the show and retreats when Democratic policies run the show.

Further the already significant disparity between Republican GDP growth and Democratic GDP growth found in the data compiled in comparing control to GDP may mask an even greater disparity. In the 36 years between 1981 and 2017, with Republican low tax policies dominating, the net GDP gain was 71.62%. During those years Government consistently spent more money than it brought in, the National debt rose about 70% (from 31% of GDP in 1981 to somewhere over 100% of GDP in 2017). The total net GDP "gain" from 1981 to 2017 almost exactly matches the increased debt burden the country assumed.

This suggests virtually all the GDP increase over those years wasn't a function of policy being managed efficiently by savvy Republican business folks, it was stealing growth from future generations who will have to pay off that debt. Additional factors only compound the inexplicable lack of real growth

As discussed in prior chapters, economists have found that GDP rises faster when a bigger percentage of the population is in their prime working years. This period since 1981 coincides almost perfectly with the period when one of the largest populations of working folks in US history were in the job market in their prime productive years (about 30 to 55 years old).[47] The leading edge of the huge explosion in births that occurred after World War II, the baby boomers, were moving into their thirties in the early 1980's and spent their productive years governed by policies reflecting Republican ideology. Yet GDP "gain" for that period is almost perfectly offset by the increased National Debt.

Beginning in the 1970's more and more women were moving into the workforce (not that say at home homemakers weren't an important factor in the economy, but they weren't a factor that counted for much in GDP figures). Women moving into the workforce should have added another boost to productivity from more workers.

Take away the GDP boost from constant deficit spending and the GDP boost from the most favorable demographics in modern history, one can't rule out the possibility the GDP growth since 1982 would have been negative. The curious correlations between Republican control and income inequality and CEO pay are entirely consistent with the notion the economy wasn't really growing. It was redistributing wealth by incurring government debt to allow the wealthiest taxpayers to stash away more wealth.

---

[47] https://www.investopedia.com/articles/investing/012315/how-demographics-drive-economy.asp

Chapter 29
Making Sense of These Curious Correlations

How do we explain these curious correlations that in some instances contradict public perception?

That a correlation exists between low tax rates and a growing National Debt is not unexpected, even though it contradicts Republican belief lowering taxes on the wealthy sparks economic growth. Did Republicans believe that? Or was that notion just wishful thinking to justify what they saw as a need for increased defense spending? It's simple common sense we can all relate to from managing our own finances, less money coming in means either lowering expenses or incurring debt. If you are increasing expenses and decreasing income you are going to incur debt.

The correlation between very high tax rates on the top end of the income of the wealthiest taxpayers and higher GDP growth is probably counterintuitive for nearly everyone. It contradicts conventional wisdom that is in part rooted in the rules we all use to manage our budgets.

How can higher taxes spark an increase in growth? Perhaps these other curious correlations identified provide a clue.

The correlation between high taxes on the wealthiest taxpayers and income distribution for example. When taxes on the wealthiest incomes were high, workers incomes rose, putting more of the wealth the economy generated in the hands of workers who spend what they earn rather than investing in safe wealth storage. That same logic fits comfortably with the correlation between skyrocketing CEO pay in comparison to stagnant worker pay.

The correlation between high taxes and asset bubbles and low stock market returns suggest that when taxes on the top end of the wealthiest taxpayers' income are low, large amounts of new wealth generated flows into existing assets and drives up prices beyond historical norms. We end up with overpriced stocks and lower growth.

The correlation between high taxes on the wealthiest taxpayers and stability in the housing market seems related to both rising incomes by workers and a lack of speculative asset bubbles.

Chapter 30
It's Not About the People

There is no biological reason to believe Democrats are smarter than Republicans. Politicians can seldom afford to be wise about long term consequences - they live in a rough and tumble world of short-term expediency. To survive they make decisions on the fly trying to balance whether they can keep a majority of their voters happy even if that means mistreating a minority. Their policy wisdom cannot generally exceed the wisdom of the majority of the voters in their constituency.

This suggests the problem is ideological. Adopting philosophical notions to avoid having to analyze every little issue that comes up.

Republicans tend to celebrate the individual and downplay the community, an ideology that in United States has been handed down from a long history of pushing into uncharted frontier where law was often what you made it and being capable of living self sufficiently was a necessity.

Today that ideology is comfortable for some wealthy people as it protects their wealth and limits their responsibility to the community. Although that describes a small portion of voters, they are people who have money to spend, know marketing and can sell their ideas to folks who would otherwise vote differently if they understood their best economic interests.

But, as these curious correlations reveal, Republican dislike for government interference in the market has resulted, when Republicans control the levers of government for extended periods of time, in repeated bouts of turning a blind eye to excessive speculation, exploitation and even fraud. At a point market collapses result in major dislocation in the economy that affect rich and poor alike, but with a more devastating impact on those who have little.

Democratic ideology tends to see the community as more important (it takes a village and all that). They see themselves as more attuned to who is not doing as well in the market, although history has shown they can in fact be pretty oblivious to the plight of working folks.

Democrats better historical economic performance probably in part relates to their constituency making them more aware of negative motivations driving the market and Democrats have been willing to use government to steer the market away from excess. But it seems unlikely the Democrats realized high tax rates on the wealthy would correlate with better GDP growth. When they imposed high rates by all appearances it was just to avoid running up the National Debt in World War I, then the Great Depression and then World War II. The only folks with the money to pay off the debt without crippling consumption were the very wealthy.

The fact suggested by the data that precedes this chapter that overall wealth of the country increases faster when income is spread more broadly across the society was an inadvertent by-product of the need to generate revenue, plus pursuing policies that supported higher wages, unemployment insurance and other distributive programs that kept money in circulation to support the economy.

Democratic superior GDP numbers are also probably a byproduct of the increasing complexity of our economic life.

If you were unhappy 150 years ago you moved west and homesteaded on 140 acres of Government land, got a free mule from the government and were set to build a life. Republican notions of small government and self-sufficiency made a lot of sense to those folks (even though it was not a small government that was handing out land and mules for free). That is no longer an option. Even the surviving family farmers are no longer self-sufficient. Increasingly the linked and interdependent community is the future.

So why aren't Democrats still in power? Why, after controlling Congress for 24 years could Ronald Reagan come in and sell the idea Democrats and big government were the nations problem?

Democrats had ignored two very real problems that come to mind pretty quickly.

Labor Unions are bad solution to a very real problem. Labor Unions are an offshoot of the dog eat dog world of an unregulated market. Labor Unions arose in response to exploitation of workers by management locked in the market driven race to the bottom. Since government was unwilling to even see it as a problem the only way workers could get traction was through concerted effort to thwart production - hit the owners in the pocketbook.

Later, when government started paying more attention, instead of attempting to find a more creative solution to the race to the bottom problem, government simply legalized the adversarial attitude that used the threat of thwarted production to protect workers. But Labor Unions are subject to the same negative motivations that bedevil a free market. Labor Unions can evolve into mini dictatorships serving the needs of the labor union bosses and oblivious to the health of the businesses that employs their members.

Nor have current Democrats shown any awareness of a need to change the adversarial relationship between management and labor to allow companies to be a team working for a common goal rather that two sides squabbling to divide up the pie. (Republicans are barely aware there is a race to the bottom problem).

The second big Democratic policy failure was they did not have the foresight to index tax brackets. Congress would hash out tax brackets and rates at some point in time then those brackets would be in place for, in some cases, decades. So over time natural inflation would, fortuitously for Congress, increase revenue as inflation moved people into high tax brackets even as their real income was not increasing.

In the late 1960's through the 1970's unusually high inflation pushed lots of middle-income people whose real incomes hadn't changed much into higher tax brackets. It was politically convenient as the Treasury received more revenue without that embarrassing need to publicly raise taxes. But the Democratic Congress was oblivious to basic fairness and set the stage for the decades of anti-tax Republicans who have followed.

The 1964 changes to the tax rates by a Democratic Congress with a Democratic President represent evidence Democrats did not realize the behavioral modification value of very high tax rates. The 1964 tax changes brought the top income tax rate down to around 70%, undermining much of the value 90% tax rates had in encouraging the top 1% to keep money in productive assets. But it didn't address the fact a bigger percentage of the not quite so wealthy population were now paying 70% on some portion of their income because inflation was pushing them into higher tax brackets.

If we put aside the notion either Republicans or Democrats have cornered the market on wisdom, how can you explain these correlations?

Let's speculate a bit.

Section F

Speculation and Ideas for Change

    Chapter 31 - Surplus Income

    Chapter 32 - How Do We Change the Future?

    Chapter 33 - Test Economic Opinions with Data

    Chapter 34 - Speculation - Specific Policy Changes

    Chapter 35 - Valuing These Curious Correlations

Chapter 31

Surplus Income

How can higher tax rates on the wealthiest taxpayers generate a stronger national economy? Here is a possible explanation.

"Surplus" Income" - A research study from a few years ago found that the average person thinks they would be happy with income of $70,000 to $90,000 a year.[48]

Who knows how accurate that figure is, but the concept of the study is useful. Individual perceptions of when income becomes "surplus" probably vary considerably across a population, but most of us intuitively would accept the idea that for all but the most unusual person there is an income level at which all of a person's wants or needs are met so any extra income in a particular year is "surplus".

What is a person with "surplus" income going to do with that money? Probably, like a squirrel hiding acorns, find some way to stash it way for the future.

If they try to start a new business it means taking on a lot of work, and a lot of risk of losing the money, not to mention a distraction upsetting their comfortable life.

Most people are not going to want to go that route.

Instead they will invest it in some existing asset - stocks or bonds or real estate usually. Or maybe they will indulge a passion by buying a 1957 Ferrari

---

[48] https://www.marketwatch.com/story/this-is-exactly-how-much-money-you-need-to-be-truly-happy-earning-more-wont-help-2018-02-14

Testarossa, or a Van Gogh painting, or Michael Jackson's glove.

The notion of "surplus income" becomes even more compelling when people can control their income.

Controlling Your Income - The very wealthy usually control the businesses from which they derive their income. As owners or managers of the enterprise they often can control their compensation.

Corporations are a big part of modern enterprise. Corporations allow people to protect personal wealth while investing in productive enterprises. Productive enterprises are inherently risky. A change in market conditions, a mistake by an employee, a natural disaster - the possibility of catastrophic liability is always present. So wealthy people put enough money into an enterprise to control it, then fund the enterprise through debt and thereby keep their personal fortune protected from loss and pull money out of the corporation when possible.

When we consider that most of us have a point where additional income is "surplus" with the way modern business enterprise is structured we begin to see a compelling explanation for why GDP is so much better during periods of very high marginal tax rates on the wealthiest taxpayers.

When a very wealthy taxpayer is "only" being taxed at 40% on their "surplus" income they may calculate 40% is worth paying to be able to pull the money out of risky productive enterprise and stash it for the future by investing in a non productive asset, or publicly traded security (profits from which will be taxed at lower capital gains tax rates).

But when the "surplus" income is taxed at 85% or 90% the calculation probably often changes. Instead of pulling the money out of risky productive enterprises, it makes more sense to build their wealth by leaving the money in risky productive enterprises and trying to expand their enterprise portfolio.

The concept of "surplus" income can explain the plethora of asset bubbles that have cropped up in the last couple decades as income inequality increased.

Paintings by old masters that sell for double the price they sold for a few years ago, or classic cars whose prices follow a similar trajectory. Wall street consistently running up to stock valuations far beyond long-term price/earnings averages, or housing prices rising rapidly in markets where wealthy folk live.

This author never heard the words "asset bubble" in the first 20 years of his adult life when Democratic high tax policies were still in effect - except as a dimly perceived historical occurrence involving Tulips or the 1929 Stock Market crash.

With low tax rates once a very wealthy person reaches the point of "surplus" income in a particular year that "surplus" will probably not go into a productive investment that feeds the consumption machine that drives modern economies.

If that "surplus" remains in productive enterprises their expansion puts money in the hands of working folks who do not have everything they need and want. They spend most of it - consumer spending that drives new opportunities for business and productive investment.

It appears that Republican economics of low taxes on the wealthy has funneled money to Wall Street and non-productive assets at the expense of Main Street productive activity. It makes the rich comparatively very rich. But in the end the country and every person in it are poorer. [49]

---

[49] A 2021 study found the US lost 23 Trillion in growth since 1990 "Inequality Has Cost the U.S. Nearly $23 Trillion Since 1990" By Catarina Saraiva, September 8, 2021

Chapter 32
How do we Change the Future?

Winter is a dreary time in much of the world. The days are short, often uncomfortably cold. We have no control over the way the earth spins on its axis so we cannot control winter. As a culture we have learned to deal with winters dreary nature. Some move south in winter to avoid the cold and short days. For most of us we rely on what our entrepreneurial nature has developed to make winter bearable. Housing that is warm and full of light, music and entertainment in winter. We have created holidays, focused our primary shopping season in winter and filled winter with sporting events.

Unlike winter, the market is not beyond our control. It is entirely a function of our inherent patterns of thinking. We are capable of shaping it once we understand it.

We often speak as if great leaders are the strength of our country. However, history suggests peace, prosperity and stability in a country usually doesn't come from the leaders, it comes from the citizens/voters being wise enough to find the right leaders.

There are always political leaders who are clever enough to say what people want to hear and have the charm and demeanor to inspire confidence and enthusiasm. They often are so focused on their personal goals and prejudices they are ignorant of what is actually good for the country. Hitler, Mussolini, Fidel Castro, or Hugo Sanchez/Nicholas Maduro - a few extreme examples that come readily to mind.

The modern media landscape has aggravated this weakness for choosing leaders based on glib slogans and superficial appearances by giving politicians astonishing amounts of information about what people emotionally want to hear, how they should seek to appear in public and how they can manipulate public opinion.

Politics will always attract empire builders. A better political future hinges less on wiser leaders than it does on wiser citizens. Voters caring enough about making informed decisions in the voting booth to take a little time out of their life to look beyond platitudes and appearances.

Understanding the curious correlations explored in this book are a start. It puts an exclamation point on the fact good policy is usually complex, particularly economic police. Politicians and pundits often exaggerate for simplicity. But here are some basic rules for a modern voter we can glean from these curious correlations.

Be suspicious when a politician or pundit:

1. Presents economic policy as a choice between raw capitalism and socialism/communism. That is a false choice; the spectrum of options existing to manage the free market and take advantage of its strengths while minimizing the damage of its weaknesses is limited only by rear view mirror thinking.

2. Proposes tax changes that would open the housing market to create opportunity for speculators. Good housing policy should value stability and homeowner access over creating opportunities for speculation that simply reallocates existing wealth.

3. Proposes "market" solutions to improve the Health care industry. In an increasingly mobile world where disease can spread across the world in a matter of

hours, we are all at risk when people do not have health care. But history has demonstrated quality health care for all is fundamentally incompatible with a profit motive driven corporate health care market. Profit will always trump health in crunch time. (Perhaps competing non-profit organizations might offer a solution)

4. Proposes increasing the National Debt to hand out tax cuts to voters. That's not unlike handing out bags of candy to your grandchildren every time you see them so they will like you. Effective but not wise. Tax cuts also usually result in pennies in savings for working people and bags of money for the people that will stash it away in non-productive assets.

5. Proposes tax cuts to free up capital for investment. In the United States today we are drowning in investment capital. We don't need more capital; we need more of what we have to go into productive activity rather than inflating the value of existing assets.

Giving Tax cuts to free up capital usually involves lowering taxes on the wealthiest taxpayers - the folks who are already the most prone to put the extra money into a non-productive asset.

If your goal is a stable, safe world for you and your family encouraging the wealthiest members of the population to stash away as much wealth as possible is ignoring a history of hundreds of years of riots and war sparked by poverty leading to anger against folks who hoard too much wealth and power.

More general goals to strive for as a voter:

Think about how history informs the social and political ideas you hold, and where those ideas came from in your life. Do they actually make sense in the life you are living?

Question the orthodoxy of expert thinking. The groupthink that closes minds is not just a disease that strikes government. It is rampant in professions who use their position and expertise to control access to advancement in their profession, be they aspiring Doctors, Lawyers, PhD candidates, politicians or Wall Street bankers. They aren't evil, just being human. They work hard to climb to the top. Their ambition just didn't leave time to question the truth of orthodox thinking they had to learn to advance.

Constantly remind yourself that we are all different. We accept that without question in our physical world. Some of us are tall, some are not, some are thin, and some are not. Some have long torsos and short legs; some have long legs and shorter torsos. We differ in eye color, skin color, hair color. But we cannot visually perceive different ways of thinking so we have a hard time not assuming everybody else should think the same and respond emotionally the same as we do. If they do not think and feel like us, we feel they must be wrong or misguided. There are vast differences between individual humans in how they think and respond emotionally, in their ambitions and what they need to survive and be comfortable.

Chapter 33
Test Economic Opinions with Data

Politically it is particularly important to test economic opinions dominating the media. Economic mistakes impact us all. As this is being written we are living in a time that illustrates the need to question orthodox economic thinking.

There are many issues on which economists disagree. Some economists would agree with some of the points raised in this chapter. The following discussion is most directly applicable to the branch of economic thinking most devoted to free markets whom Republicans have relied upon for the last couple decades to justify their tax and economic policy choices.

Those high-profile Economists have been baffled by economic circumstances since the Great Recession. The ideological tools they use to understand what is happening in the economy have lost their predictive value. In classic economics in the Pre Covid-19 days when unemployment hovered around historic lows, the economy should be robust and wages rising. But the economy was mediocre, despite trillions in deficit spending by the government, and the evidence suggests the only real increases in wages may not be market driven, but a result of many local and state governments enacting substantial increases in the minimum wage.

The parable of the 12 blind men each hanging onto a bit of an elephant is illustrative. Each experienced a different elephant but they all assume what they extrapolate from their experience is all they need to know to understand the elephant.

Economist self-select. The economists whom Republican ideology relied upon probably become economists because they place a high value on wealth as a primary goal in life, and are more comfortable viewing logic and math as reality rather than as an imperfect tool to understand reality. While they may quibble about small details, they reinforce one another's basic perceptual blind spots.

They bury us in the data they develop to the point it is incomprehensible to folks who don't want to take the time to sort it all out, so voters and politicians defer to their apparent expertise.

Yet as the current economy demonstrates their perceptual blind spots sometimes make them incapable of putting all the pieces of their own data together if it contradicts their worldview of how people should think and behave. They were baffled by why prior to the Covid-19 economy, with unemployment around 4%, wage growth was anemic.

They should ask 4% of what? According to the Bureau of Labor Statistics[50] in late 2006 about 63.5% of the population was working. Since the Great Recession that figure has been mostly below 60%. As a percentage of the population that amounts to nearly 10,000,000 fewer folks working today than were working in late 2006. In the first decade or so after the bottom of the great Recession when unemployment was at 19% in late 2009 the number of folks working rose only about 1%. The unemployment rate wasn't low because we have a good economy or were engaging in wise economic policies, it

---

[50] https://www.bls.gov/opub/ted/2016/mobile/employment-population-ratio-59-point-7-percent-unemployment-rate-4-point-7-percent-in-may.htm

was low because a lot of people were pushed out of the job market.

The Great Recession could have turned into a Great Depression if it weren't for the fact many of the workers who lost their job were old enough to turn to retirement accounts or Social Security so the consumer base of the economy did not collapse. Wages have stagnated for nearly 40 years so few of those who stepped out of the job market saw any reason to get back in.

Some economists continue to cite modest rises in wages in the last couple years as a sign the free market is working and we are on our way back, totally ignoring the major increase in the minimum wage mandated by state and local governments beginning in about 2013. In much of the country the minimum wage has nearly doubled in six years.

Most private economists, and certainly those whose opinions make it to the media, have always been either academics or employed by big corporations. Their world often involves Wall Street, not Main Street. They are immersed in the Wall Street groupthink driven by folks who do not distinguish between trading and actually producing something. They tend to talk to the media about the data that fits their worldview and overlook the data that is inconvenient.

Much of classic economic theory is rooted in the belief economic systems will only work by accommodating to the desires of most ambitious, acquisitive and self-centered – the empire builders whose lives are devoted to accumulating economic and/or political power. They assume, as a quote attributed to a former head of General Motors stated, "What's good for General Motors is good for America".[51]

---

[51] https://en.wikiquote.org/wiki/Charles_Erwin_Wilson

Even if that means General Motors plans to lay some people off to improve their profit margin, or outsource part of their production overseas?

History has demonstrated that economic systems controlled by, or that cater to, those members single mindedly devoted to accumulating economic/political power are inefficient systems that create vast disparities in the distribution of wealth, even as they make the overall society less productive than it could be with a broader distribution of wealth through society. Not to mention they tend to foster wars and revolutions.

We need to respect the right of people to be ambitious, acquisitive or self-centered. But we need to balance their right to pursue their goals against the impact their activities have on others with a government that sets up rules of engagement that preclude exploitation, values production over trade, and controls speculation. The economic theories politicians have relied on for the last 40 years has done a poor job of meeting that goal.

Chapter 34

Speculating on Specific Policy Changes

Taxes: Back in the 1970's and early 1980's when the argument was being advanced to eliminate very high tax rates on very high levels of income the argument that prevailed was that very few people actually paid the high rates so they generated very little income for government.

Suppose that the very high rates were causing more wealth to remain in productive activity, which increased GDP and thereby increased governments take at lower income levels? That could explain how those "tax and spend" Democrats managed to produce high GDP growth at the same time they paid down the national debt.

Suppose we stop thinking of taxes as simple revenue generation? Suppose we start thinking taxes can also be a behavior modification tool to address the weaknesses in the unregulated free market? Use taxes as carrots and sticks. Bring in some of the behavioral modification techniques already widely used in other professions.

We could bring back very high tax rates on the upper end of the income of the very wealthy to encourage keeping wealth in productive investment. An efficient Congress would set up some scale that was indexed for inflation so people whose income was really not increasing would not be jumping into higher tax brackets because of inflation. Use brackets that reflect where folks stand in the percentage of relative income, then the IRS could adjust the brackets each year to take inflation (or deflation) into account.

We could bring back the provisions in the 1954 Tax Code that allowed people to average their income over 5 years so the newly wealthy had time to accumulate a little more before the higher tax rates apply.

We could compliment the high rates by not unduly rewarding speculation in existing assets, the kind of speculation that produces no new good or service and tends to destabilize markets. Eliminate the Capital Gains tax and tax income from the sale of assets as ordinary income. But to be fair we then would need to allow a deduction that would adjust for inflation. If you bought a farm and worked it for 30 years, the farm you bought 30 years ago for $1000 might sell now for $30,000, but some or all of that gain is simply inflation. So, you adjust the sales price for inflation before you determine if there is a taxable gain.

To simplify the tax computation, allow people to invest their securities in a securities trust account where gains or losses from buying and selling are not taxed, the gain is only taxed when money is withdrawn from the account. The tax is computed by applying the inflation factor applicable to the entire account to the amount coming out to account for gain that is simply inflation.

We could bring back the law repealed in 1995 that allows people to sell their house and buy a new house with no tax consequences as long as all the money from the old house goes into the new house. Help regular people build wealth for retirement while removing incentives for speculation in the residential real estate market.

Corporations:

First by-pass archaic state law by setting up requirements that make public policy sense for corporations. Require for tax purposes strict disclosure of ownership from corporations that own interests in other corporations and that all corporations linked by ownership be treated as one taxable entity.

Then turn the current corporate tax scheme on its head. Instead of taxing corporate income as a matter of course, we tax money coming out of the corporation. Encourage keeping money in the pool for risky investment by making the basic rule corporate income is not taxed. Then we can use a corporate tax in specific situations where there is some other policy goal to be achieved.

For example, we use tax law to prevent the race to the bottom and control excessive CEO pay by setting up mathematical relationships between the top earners and the bottom earners within the Corporation, similar to the Federal Government salary classification system.

A corporation can pay more, or less than the Federal government scale but the relationship of the top to the bottom must remain within the parameters set by law. If a corporation attempts to gain competitive advantage through exploitation of the less skilled workers so the gap between the top earners and the bottom earners becomes excessive the Corporation starts incurring income taxes. The taxes will hurt profitability, which will make the corporation a less appealing investment and offset any competitive advantage gained over market rivals. Let tax policy work with the market to avoid the race to the bottom.

This policy could also change the relationship between labor and management. Increases in labor salaries would follow with corporate success for which management seeks a reward. The corporation becomes a team working to benefit all.

Chapter 35
Valuing These Curious Correlations

As noted in the beginning of this volume, science does not generally consider correlation as proof. This works as a policy for the hard sciences such as physics and chemistry that can be understood with observation and mathematical computation. The basic laws of the universe at this point in our understanding seem to be amenable to identification through these two tools and we have made huge strides toward understanding the Universe, in part because we are disinterested observers.

Once we start studying ourselves observation and mathematical computation have proved to be insufficient tools in the social sciences. We do statistically based studies on behavior and have learned a lot about what the average human thinks and does, but we have no reliable way to understand and predict what any individual will think or do, and the average may mask huge disparities in behavior.

It may be that we as a species turn out to be the most complex system in the universe. But studying ourselves may also be part of the problem as our individual differences in thinking shape perceptions.

Let's talk common sense. Politicians use the term frequently. Let's assume it means knowledge that is not just what experts say, but all the knowledge we gather as humans about what works and what doesn't work in life.

Consider two professions, economics and teaching. Suppose our life experience suggests the type of people that go into economics are generally focused on numbers and money, and maybe not inclined to spend much time attuned to other people, perhaps even lacking in some people skills. They make decisions based on ...well, economics. Life is a calculation.

Whereas the people who go into teaching are obviously not primarily attuned to money - you won't get rich teaching. Their calculation tips toward the rewards of human interaction.

Science cannot explain why one person becomes an economist while another becomes a teacher. But common sense has no problem accepting these two basic personality characterizations as generally true, because common sense is rooted in life experience, not what can be statistically proven.

Yet the economics profession beliefs and theories are rooted in the assumption everybody thinks (or should think) like an economist.

Common sense was the title of a publication that was influential in leading up to the Declaration of Independence, expounding the philosophy that led to an entirely new form of Government being fashioned as the United States.[52] Thomas Paine could not prove his ideas were true. But his ideas meshed with and clarified what life experience had taught our forefathers they wanted out of life.

The data found in these curious correlations is rooted in historical fact. It is time to apply a little common sense.

---

[52] For background see the wikipedia annotation on "Common Sense (pamphlet)"

Ronald Reagan is the face of modern Republican economic theory involving low taxes on the wealthy, high defense spending and little concern for the federal deficit.

On the campaign trail Reagan once said (about Democrats) that the definition of insanity was doing the same thing over and over and expecting different results.[53]

For nearly four decades Republican economic ideas rooted in tax cuts and catering to the wealthy have dominated federal public policy. After four decades our net gain as a country, subtracting debt incurred from GDP growth, is effectively zero per year. The rich have gotten a lot richer, while the poor get poorer and many working folks can't expect to own a home unless they inherit it from their parents. For four decades we have been transferring wealth to rich folks without actually growing economically.

Common sense has to say, well yes, we have continued to do the same thing and expect different results, and it has been a little crazy.

---

[53] A comment also attributed to Albert Einstein among others - https://quoteinvestigator.com/2017/03/23/same/

Appendix A- Historical Narrative

Year-by-year control, GDP and National Debt

As an initial caveat - I am not a mathematician, statistician or any other kind of math person. I found math mostly boring in school although as an adult I have found it sometimes useful. I have made the computations in this book using my meager math skills - but the results are so striking I have considerable confidence that they reflect reality. Virtually all the data sources utilized are available to anyone on the Internet. I invite you to do your own computations if you find it hard to accept what the data says, perhaps using the resources from the Bureau of Economic Analysis at the Commerce Department (https://apps.bea.gov)

About the Data

Taxation Data - For this survey we make a note of the percentage of tax applicable to the highest incomes on the assumption it is broadly representative of the trend in taxation for each period. (See the Chapters on taxation for more detailed, although still greatly simplified information).

GDP Data Quirks - GDP data was drawn from public Internet sources: That includes raw GDP numbers as well as the inflation-adjusted growth in GDP we primarily rely upon. We refer to GDP, but the figure was actually measured as Gross National Product (GNP) until 1990. GDP and GNP are very similar so we will be using them interchangeably, with the more modern nomenclature of GDP as the norm.

Because data from before 1940 is not as readily available, we use GDP figures from a number of different sources and the exact GDP figures vary significantly depending on the underlying assumptions used by the sources in computing GDP.

As an example, the data from the website "Social Democracy" was the source for pre-1930 information and for consistency was used through 2001 (the last year available from that source). Since 2001 GDP computations were derived from "multpl.com". "Social Democracy" computes GDP growth for 1978 at 4.58%. Multpl.com computes 1978 at 6.68%. Using the multpl.com numbers would flatter Democrats. Compare the same sites for 1979 and they compute 2.26% v. 1.30% where the "Social Democracy" numbers are more favorable to Democrats. In 1980 the "Social Democracy number is less flattering for Democrats -1.12% compared to -0.4% in the multipl.com compilation.

Or with the older years, multpl.com cites 1933 GDP growth as -26.34%, again it would greatly lower the Republican numbers, while "Social Democracy", the number we use, computes 1933 GDP at -2.6%.

Consider the numbers presented here as representative of the trend rather than an exact reflection of a very complex reality.

As noted in the main volume text we look at GDP figures for the years a party actually controls the levers of Government and do the same with a 1-year offset on the assumption the first year of any Congressional Session the credit or blame for GDP figures is more accurately assigned to the party that controlled the prior Congress.

Detailed Control, GDP and National Debt Data
1919 to 1932 - Republican Control

This era was marked by a net loss of GDP and a net rise in the National Debt. GDP in 1918 was 75.8 billion and in 1932 59.5 billion. The National Debt started in 1918 at about 30% of GDP and ended in 1932 at 39% of GDP.

1919 to 1920 - Republicans captured majorities in both houses of Congress in the election of November of 1918. Republicans had a single vote majority in the Senate (48 to 47) and a substantial majority in the House (237 to 191). Although the Democratic President, Woodrow Wilson had two years left on his second term, Wilson was consumed by his efforts to create a League of Nations, traveling to Paris then barnstorming the US to drum up support for the idea before suffering a debilitating stroke in October of 1919, six months after the new Republican Congress began their terms. From March of 1919 when the Republican majorities took office through 1920 the Republican Congress was relatively unencumbered by the President from the other party. **GDP** - Prohibition was approved in 1918. The end of World War I produced rampant inflation followed by short, deep recession. GDP took a big drop due to the demobilization of the war effort that began in 1919 coupled with the impact of prohibition - the alcohol industry, the 5th largest industry in the United States, shut down. Although in 1918 GDP was 75.8 billion and in 1920 it was 88.4 billion, the inflation adjusted GDP was .037% in 1919 and -4.12% in 1920. Using a one-year offset Inflation adjusted GDP was -2.25% in 1920 and -4.12% in 1921.

Tax Rate - The top income tax rate was 73%.

National Debt: The debt peaked in 1919 at about 34.5% of GDP. By the end of 1921 it was 32% of GDP, a net debt reduction of -1.25% per year.

1921 through 1932 - Republicans control all three elective power centers for all but the 1931-1932 session when they had 2/3rds control. In 1931-32 Republicans had a one-vote majority in the Senate but were tied with the Democrats in the House. The Democrats aligned with the single progressive party member to have a slight advantage in the House.

Tax Rates: With a Republican Congress and Presidents (Harding, Coolidge and Hoover) Congress passes a series of tax cuts between 1921 and 1929, dropping the top income tax rate from 73% to 25% and granting Capital Gains special tax treatment for the first time. The highest tax rate rose to 63% for 1932 (Democrats retroactively enacted the change in 1933).

GDP: 1921 - 1932 Inflation adjusted GDP averaged -.8% per year. 1922-1933 1-year offset inflation adjusted GDP averaged -1.19% per year.

National Debt: The debt dropped from about 32% of GDP in 1922 to 16% of GDP in 1929 then rose to 39% of GDP by 1933 for a net debt increase as a percentage of GDP of 7%, an average debt increase of 0.58% per year over 12 years.

1933 through 1946 - Democratic Congress and the Presidents

1933 through 1941 - Democrats controlled all three branches of government with large majorities in both the House and Senate from March of 1933 through 1946. In this period prior to World War II the Democratic Congress and President (Roosevelt) began in early 1933 mired in the Great Depression, with unemployment at 25%. Roosevelt and Congress enacted numerous programs over the next few years to put people to work. The incoming Congress in 1933 immediately raised the highest tax bracket from 25% to 63% making it retroactive so the new rates were applied to 1932 tax returns taxpayers were preparing to file. By 1941 the highest tax rate was 81%.

GDP - 1933-1941 inflation adjusted GDP gained 8% per year. Applying the offset 1934-1942 average GDP gain was 8.45% per year.

National debt - The debt was 40% of GDP in 1934 and rose to 45% of GDP in 1941 for a net debt increase of .83% per year over 6 years.

1942 through 1946 - During World War II Democrats continued to hold Congress and the Presidency (Roosevelt and Truman). Some preparation for war began before Pearl Harbor but massive mobilization began after December 7, 1941. In the demobilization after the war ended GDP took a big hit as government expenditures were drastically reduced, post war recession begins in late 1945. The top tax rate went from 79% to 94% by 1945 then down to 91% for 1946-1947.

GDP - 1942-1946 inflation adjusted GDP was 2.35%. 1-year offset (1943 to 1947) the average inflation adjusted GDP was -0.9135% per year.

National Debt - The debt was 48% of GDP in 1942 and climbed to a peak of 119% in 1946 then dropped to 104% of GDP by 1947. Net debt increase of about +11.2% per year over five years.

Although for the next 34 years control occasionally flipped briefly to Republicans, Democratic policies developed by FDR prevailed - evidenced by continued high tax rates and no major changes in the New Deal programs.

1947 and 1948 - In the wake of the Post World War II economic downturn Republicans enjoyed a two-year period controlling both houses of Congress with significant numbers advantages in both Houses. But with a Democratic President and a large debt from World War II there was little change in policy direction. The Postwar Marshall plan was developed to help Europe recover as the Cold War begins.

GDP - 1947-1948 inflation adjusted GDP averaged growth of .34%. 1948-1949 1-year offset inflation adjusted GDP was 2.01% in 1948 and -1.33% in 1949 for an average GDP growth of .34% per year

The top tax rate remained at 91%.

National Debt - in 1947 the debt was 104% of GDP, by 1949 it had fallen to 93% of GDP. - Net debt decrease of about -5.5% per year over 2 years.

1949 through 1952 - Democrats had 4 years of complete control with comfortable margins other than a single seat difference in the Senate in 1951-52 and a Democratic President (Truman). The Cold War spins off the Korean War.

GDP - 1949 through 1952 inflation adjusted GDP averaged 4.35% per year. For 1950 to 1953 1-year offset inflation adjusted GDP averaged 4.38% per year.

Tax Rates - The top tax rate remained at 91% then went up to 92% for 1952.

National Debt: In 1950 the debt was 89% of GDP. It fell to 68% of GDP in 1953 for a net debt decrease of about -5.25% per year over 4 years.

1953-1954 - Republicans controlled all three elective power centers, but with modest majorities (Senate 48 to 46, House 221 to 213). Much of Congressional energy from 1951 through 1954 went into the McCarthy hearings to search and destroy alleged communists. With a moderate Republican President (Eisenhower), the Korean War approaching a stalemate and the National debt still very high there was no major change in the Democratic policies enacted in the previous 20 years.

Tax Rates: In 1954 Congress accomplished a major repeal and reenactment of the Internal Revenue Code but it carried forward the basic tax scheme that had been in place since the Great Depression and the top tax rate remained at 92%.

GDP: After fighting wound down in Korea there was an ensuing economic slowdown. 1953-54 Inflation adjusted GDP averaged growth of 1.4% per year.1-year offset 1954-1955 inflation adjusted GDP was 1.4% per year.

National Debt: Debt was 68% of GDP in 1953 and 65% in 1955 for a net debt decrease of -1.5% per year over two years.

1955 through 1981 - Democratic Control

For this 26-year span Democrats held both houses of Congress, although the Presidency switched back and forth between the parties. From 1955 to 1960 with a Republican President (Eisenhower) the Democratic advantage was modest. From 1961 to 1980 the Democratic majorities in Congress were large. From 1961 to 1968 Congress worked with Democratic Presidents (Kennedy and Johnson). From 1969 to 1976 the Democratic Congress worked with two Republican Presidents (Nixon and Ford). From 1977 to 1980 Congress worked with a Democratic President (Carter). The inflation adjusted average GDP for that 26-year period was 2.09% per year and the National debt dropped further each year, by 1981 it was down to 31% of GDP.

1955 through 1960 - A Democratic Congress and Republican President (Eisenhower) as Sputnik launch by Russia sparks US space technology spending.

GDP: 1955-1960 Inflation adjusted GDP grew .78% per year. Using the 1-year offset 1956 to 1961 inflation adjusted GDP grew .78% per year.

Tax Rates: The top tax rate dropped to 91%.

National Debt: The debt stood at 65% of GDP in 1955 and 52% in 1961 for a net debt decrease of about -2.16% per year over 6 years.

1961 through 1968 - A Democratic Congress and Presidents (Kennedy and Johnson) during a continued expansion of space program and escalation of the war in Vietnam

GDP: 1961-1968 Inflation adjusted GDP grew 3.64% annually. 1-year offset 1962 to 1969 inflation adjusted GDP grew 3.64% annually.

Tax Rates: The top tax rate was at 91% until in 1964 it dropped to 77%, then to 70% in 1965.

National Debt: The debt was 52% of GDP in 1961 and dropped to 35% of GDP in 1969 for a Net debt decrease of about -2.25% per year over 8 years.

1969 through 1976 - A Democratic Congress and Republican Presidents (Nixon, Ford) during a period dominated by the Vietnam War. President Nixon imposes wage/price controls in an attempt to control inflation; OPEC restricts oil supplies to drive up gas prices.

Tax Rates: The top tax rate stayed at 70%.

GDP: 1969 through 1976 inflation adjusted GDP averaged 1.87% per year. 1970 to 1977 inflation adjusted GDP averaged 1.87% per year.

National Debt: In 1969 GDP was 35%, by 1977 dropped to 33% of GDP for a net debt decrease of about -.25% per year over 8 years.

1977 through 1980 - Democratic Congress and President (Carter). Inflation continued to rise. The Federal Reserve begins aggressive interest rate rises that eventually tame inflation. Iran takes US Embassy employees hostage.

GDP: 1977-80 Inflation adjusted GDP was 1.85% per year. 1977 to 1981 average inflation adjusted GDP was 1.85% per year.

Tax Rates: The top Tax rate remained at 70%.

National Debt: Debt was 33% of GDP in 1977 and 31% of GDP in 1981. Net debt reduction of -.5% per year over 4 years.

1981 to the Present - Republican tax policies dominate

Since 1981 Republican basic economic policies enacted by Ronald Reagan have dominated. The highest tax rate dropped and stayed between 25% and 40%. The National Debt has risen from 31% of GDP to about 106% of GDP

1981 through 1986 - Republicans gained a majority in the Senate and with a popular President (Ronald Reagan) pushed a Republican agenda of tax cuts, reducing regulations and increasing defense spending. Democrats continued to hold a substantial majority in the House. A major increase in defense spending springs resulted from Reagan's aggressive response to the Cold War. Savings and Loan Crisis arising from reduced regulatory oversight of the Savings and Loan Industry leads to many home foreclosures.

GDP: 1981-1986 Inflation adjusted GDP for 1981-86 averaged 2.47% per year. 1982 to 1987 per year average inflation adjusted GDP was 2.47%.

Tax Rates: The top tax rate dropped to 50%.

National Debt: Debt in 1981 was 31% of GDP. In 1987 the National Debt was 48% of GDP. Net debt increases of +2.8% per year over 6 years.

1987 through 1992 - Democrats regain control of Congress with substantial majorities in both the House and the Senate but with Republican Presidents (Reagan and GH Bush) no significant deviation from the Reagan agenda. The Soviet Union collapses, followed by the first Iraq War. Republican power brokers begin demanding Republican candidates sign a no new taxes pledge.

Tax Rates: The top tax rate dropped to 38.5% for 1987, then to 28% for 1988-1990, then up to 31% for 1991 and 1992.

GDP: 1987-1992 Inflation adjusted GDP averaged 1.26% per year. 1988 to 1993 inflation adjusted GDP averaged 1.28% per year.

National Debt: Debt in 1987 was 48% of GDP. The debt in 1993 stood at 63% of GDP. Net debt increases of +2.33% over 6 years.

1993 to 1994 - Democrats regain control of all three elective power centers. No major change from the Reagan agenda as the Democrats focused on an unsuccessful attempt to enact universal Health Care.

GDP: 1993-94 inflation adjusted GDP grew an average of 2.12% per year. 1994-1995 inflation adjusted GDP grew an average of 2.13% per year.

Tax Rates: The top tax rate was bumped slightly to 39.6% effective in 1993.

National Debt: Debt in 1993 stood at 63% of GDP and in 1995 was 64% of GDP. Net debt increases of .5% per year.

1995 through 2000 - Republicans regain control of both houses of Congress but face a Democratic President (Clinton). Bill Clinton spends his time fighting off impeachment while Republican economic reforms reduce taxes and regulations. Clinton signs off on Congressional push for deregulating financial markets.

GDP: Inflation adjusted GDP in 1995-2000 grew 2.23% per year. 1996-2001 inflation adjusted GDP grew 2.23% per year

Tax Rates: Congress pushes more Reagan agenda. Although Clinton budgets maintain the top tax rate at 39.6% the Republican Congress double down on their belief tax cuts would spark growth by lowering capital gains and other investment tax rates.

National Debt: Debt in 1995 was 64% of GDP and by 2001 debt drops to 54% of GDP for a net debt reduction of -1.66% per year over 6 years.

2001 through 2006 - Republicans control all three elective power centers, with brief periods of ambiguity in the Senate. George Bush continues with Reagan policy of increased defense spending and tax and regulatory cuts. The 9/11 attacks in 2001 led to wars in Afghanistan and Iraq with accompanying increased defense spending.

GDP: 2001-2006 inflation adjusted GDP averaged 2.8% per year. 2002 to 2007 inflation adjusted GDP averaged 2.78% per year.

Tax Rates: The top tax rate dropped from 39.6% to 35%.

National Debt: In 2001 the debt stood at 54% of GDP. By 2007 the National debt was 61% of GDP. Net debt increases of +1.16% per year over 6 years.

2007 through 2008 - Democrats win the house but Republicans continue control of the Presidency. The Senate is in flux as two independents often caucus with the Democrats. Although in numbers it was in reality more of a toss up year this compilation will treat this as a Republican controlled year since it resulted in continuation of the existing Republican policies. The Great Recession meltdown began to unfold as the Middle East wars lingered on.

GDP: 2008-2008 inflation adjusted GDP averaged -1.5% per year. 2008 through 2009 inflation adjusted GDP averaged -1.3% per year.

Tax Rate: The top tax rate remained at 35%.

National Debt: In 2007 the National debt was 61% of GDP. In 2009 it was at 83% of GDP for a net debt increases of +11% per year.

2009 through 2010 - A Democratic Congress and President (Obama) take over as the economy goes on life support (bail-out of big banks). They enact Obamacare and increased financial regulations in response to Great Recession, but no major change in Reagan era tax policies. Iraq and Afghanistan wars linger on.

GDP: 2009-2010 inflation adjusted GDP averaged 2.2% per year. 2010-2011 inflation adjusted GDP averaged 2.1% per year.

Tax Rates: Republican power brokers continue demanding candidates sign no new taxes pledge. The top tax rate remained at 35%.

National Debt: In 2009 the debt stood at 83% of GDP and in 2011 the National debt was 95% of GDP. Net debt increases of +6% per year for two years.

2011 through 2014 - With a Democratic Senate and President and Republican House little legislation occurs.

GDP: 2011-2014 inflation adjusted GDP averaged 2.165% per year. 2012 to 2015 inflation adjusted GDP averaged 2.35% per year.

Tax Rates: The top tax rate went up to 39.6% in 2013.

National Debt: In 2011 the debt was 95% of GDP and in 2015 the National Debt was 101% of GDP for a net debt increase of 1.5% per year for 4 years.

2015 through 2016 - The Republicans control Congress and Democratic President (Obama). The Middle East wars continue, the Republican Congress focuses (unsuccessfully) on repealing Obamacare.

GDP: 2015-2016 Inflation adjusted GDP averaged 2.21% per year. 2016 to 2017 inflation adjusted GDP averaged 2.35% per year.

Tax Rates: The top tax rate remains at 39.6%.

National Debt: In 2015 the debt was 101% and in 2017 the National Debt was 104% of GDP for a net debt increase of .5% per year over two years.

2017 through 2018 - A Republican Congress and President (Trump) do what Republicans always do, cut regulations and taxes?

GDP - growth in 2017 was 2.3%. Growth for 2018 was 3.2% and 1 year offset (2018-2019) yet to be determined.

Tax Rates: Top tax rate drops to 37%.

National Debt - Net debt increase of 10% according to the Congressional Budget office.

Appendix B – Tax Rate Details

Income (Wage) taxes detail - The tax on individual wage income, what we are paid for working have been changed regularly. We provide an overview below. On "wage" taxes we focus on highest tax rate and the level of income to which the highest tax rate applies at a particular time as representative of the trend in taxation. $100,000 in 1930 was a lot more wealth than $100,000 in 1976, in turn more wealth than $100,000 today so we use the comparable amount in 2018 dollars instead of the amount in actual dollars in the era being discussed.

In 1913 when the current Income Tax was enacted there were seven tax brackets. The tax did not apply until a taxpayer's **income** exceeded an amount equal to $60,000 in 2018 dollars[54] and amount above that threshold was taxed at 1%. The tax rate bumped up to a higher rate each time your income increased to the point you went into the next tax bracket. The top tax bracket in 1913 taxed at 7% applying to all your income in that year that exceeded an amount that in 2018 dollars would be $12.5 million. The tax rates rose rapidly during World War 1. When Republicans took over Congress in 1919 the top tax bracket left over from World War I was 73% on income exceeding, in 2018 dollars, about $14,000,000 per year.

---

[54] Numbers drawn from
https://www.carinsurancedata.org/calculators/inflation

Below is a chart that compares top tax rate to income it applied to at key points in time in the intervening years (again using a 2018-dollar equivalent). Keep in mind this is **yearly income**, not net wealth.

Year	Control	Top Tax Rate	Income over
1931	Republican	25%	$1,700,000
1932	Democrat	63%	$18,000,000
1945	Democrat	94%	$13,370,000
1946-1963	Democrat	91-92%	$1,655.000
1964-1981	Democrat	77%-70%	$250,000
1982-1986	Republican	50%	$108K to 180K
1987	Republican	28.5%	$97,000
1988-1991	Republican	28%	$30-35,000
1991 - 2018	Republican	31% to 39%	$66K - $425.000

The rates were never indexed for inflation, so Congress could announce they were lowering rates even as government income increased from inflation pushing more people into the higher tax brackets. This was particularly useful to politicians during the periods of high inflation in the 1970's.

Income Tax Brackets - Historically Republicans move toward fewer tax brackets and think that most wealthy taxpayers whose annual income is in the multi millions should not pay a higher rate than the highest rate paid by an upper middle-class taxpayer. Democrats have been much more comfortable with the idea of the really wealthy paying a very high percentage of the income that greatly exceeds an ordinary taxpayers' income. Democrats also allowed persons who experienced large jumps in income in a given year to average their income over the last 5 years to determine their taxes - thus the newly wealthy had a few years to build up wealth before paying the highest rates.

In 1919 when Republicans took over Congress there were 55 brackets ranging from 4% to a top rate of 73%. When they left office in 1933 the number of brackets was down to 23. Democrats immediately (before tax-day) enacted legislation changing the tax rate effective the prior year - tax year 1932. The number of tax brackets jumped back to the 55 in place from 1919 to 1921. When the Democrats lost control of tax policy in 1981 there were only 16 brackets, Republicans dropped it to 13 brackets. Over the next 36 years of Republican policy domination the number of brackets dropped as low as 2 from 1988 to 1990, rose to 7 in 2013 and dropped to 4 for 2018.

Inheritance Tax Overview

Congress tinkers with the inheritance tax less than they do with the income tax or payroll tax. For long periods the rates have stayed the same although the value of exemptions from tax fluctuated according to value of the dollar, so painting with a broad brush (using modern dollar figures) seems most useful for this volume.

1919 to 1932 - During this period of Republican control the exemption below which you did not pay tax ranged from $5 million to $14 million, the tax rate applied at the threshold was 1% and the highest tax rate applied to over $1 billion and fluctuated between 25% and 40%.

1933 to 1980 - During this period of Democratic policy dominance the exemption amount stayed around $60,000 until 1977 when it doubled. The minimum tax crept up from 1% to 3% then jumped to 18% in 1977. The top tax bracket dropped down to hit Estates over $17 million (2003 dollars) by 1981 applying a top rate over 70%.

1981 to 2018 - Republican policy regularly increased the exemption before the tax begins although this cosmetic change hasn't impacted tax revenues due to inflation; the actual amount in current dollars has remained about the same. The lowest tax rate has stayed at 18%; the top rate has dropped to 55% applicable to amounts over $17 million (2003 dollars). Billionaires no longer have a special rate.

Appendix C - Link to Data Computations

The data relied upon in computing who controlled government, tax rates and how control interacted with tax rates, GDP and the National Debt was computed using a series of data spreadsheets. They are available to view by linking to www.theidp.org and using the "more" link to go to the "Data Compilations" page. Select the folder titled "Curious Economic Correlations Data" which contains two workbooks (you may have to highlight the link and then right click to connect to the page).

"**Control and Debt**" - This workbook contains the following sheets:

Control - which summarizes by two-year congressional session increments which party controls government.

Control.yr.compute - which breaks down which party controls government by periods of unchanging basic policies.

Control.and.debt - comparing control with changes in the National Debt.

Control.Color.Code - a color-coded chart for control that largely duplicates the data in the other spreadsheets.

"**Control.GDP.and.Tax.Rates**" -contains the following sheets:

"**Control-GDP.no.offset**" - comparing GDP to which party controls government in each Congressional Session.

"**Control-GDP-1.yr.offset**" - comparing GDP to which party controls government in each Congressional Session, but offset one year to account for changes in control.

"**Tax rate-GDP**" - compares the highest marginal tax rate in a year with GDP for the year.

"**GDP-Tax rates by year**" - a more detailed breakdown of the data on control, tax rates and GDP.

Appendix D

A Brief History of Healthcare in the United States

In George Washington's time Health care was not an issue. We were a largely rural and agrarian country. Doctors were local and medical technology of the time could be purchased for relatively small amounts of money and could be carried in a satchel by a doctor on a house call. Doctor expenses were low so fees were low. They were paid in cash, or by barter.

Advances in medical knowledge and technology have driven the move toward Universal Healthcare. Even as late as the 1870's treatment for broken bones or other injuries inflicted by external forces was to have the Doctor come to the patient's house and do what they could in bandaging and splinting, then the person rested at home. Diseases were also generally treated at the victim's home, typically cutting the patient to let blood drain out of the body on the theory the blood was carrying "bad humors" (the apparent cause of George Washington's demise in his 60's after he was weakened by being out riding his farm in a cold storm all day). This wrongheaded (but inexpensive) treatment killed you pretty quickly if you were in a vulnerable physical state. If you were fundamentally healthy you probably survived. But either way no one was ill for long. Hospitals were usually only created temporarily for soldiers during war.

In short health care was primitive and ineffective - but cheap.

Then we began to learn about germs and other disease vectors. By the early 1900's European countries began creating Government Health Care systems. Teddy Roosevelt ran for President in 1912 and progressives supported him because they perceived he was open to a US Government Health Care system. But TR lost and Universal healthcare made little headway in the United States for nearly a century. Medical care (then) was still relatively cheap and inexpensive, and much of the country was still rural and self-sufficient.

But another factor in the US resisting the idea of Universal Health Care was lobbying by private interests. Doctors created a union in 1847 which was incorporated in 1897, the American Medical Association. Although the AMA has done much to improve medicine it also has vigorously opposed Universal Health Care (the AMA were the first to dub it "socialized medicine" 100 years ago).

There was a third obstacle to non -market government health care. In urban areas we started down the road to private employers providing medical insurance over 100 years ago when many employers were purchasing "sickness insurance" to care for ill or injured workers.[55] This created an Insurance industry that has a vested interest in a private system.

Today, according to study published in July of 2017 by the non-profit Commonwealth Fund[56] among the 11 most highly developed western democracies the United States ranks (as of 2014) last in the performance of its healthcare system. On a per person basis it spends significantly more than any other country. While it is in the middle of the pack (5) in rankings of the care process it is 10th or 11th in access to health care, administrative efficiency, the difference between rich and poor in treatment, and healthcare outcomes. All the

---

55 See Wikipedia - History of Health Care Reform in the United States

56 http://www.commonwealthfund.org/interactives/2017/july/mirror-mirror/ the website states "The mission of The Commonwealth Fund is to promote a high-performing health care system that achieves better access, improved quality, and greater efficiency, particularly for society's most vulnerable, including low-income people, the uninsured, minority Americans, young children, and elderly adults."

other countries have some form of coordinated national policy for Universal Health Care. Here is a summary of how we managed to be the worst of the bunch:

1919 to 1932 - Republicans Control Policy

Curiously, our VA Hospital system was expanded and consolidated during the 1920's so at that time Republicans evidently had no problem with "socialized" medicine. There was little interest in broader coverage however. Health care costs were still low, medical technology was still relatively cheap and unsophisticated so companies were willing to insure their workers and many voters were still rural and self sufficient.

1933 to 1981 - Democrats Control Policy

During the Great Depression a huge portion of the working population lost their employer coverage because they lost their jobs. In rural parts of the country people lost their self-sufficiency as they lost their farms.

Franklin Roosevelt attempted to enact a Government Health Care plan in 1935 as part of the bill that created Social Security. Opposition of the AMA jeopardized the entire legislation so the Health Care plan was dropped. The AMA evidently found traction with the Republicans who had vastly expanded the government VA hospital system 10 years earlier.

In the absence of a Government system individual hospitals began offering health insurance plans. Because the Government instituted wage and price controls during World War II employers began offering better Health Insurance plans as a way to attract employees, solidifying the foundation of our current healthcare system based on employer sponsored health care.

After World War II an act creating a National Mental Health system was enacted, and Harry Truman unsuccessfully advocated a Universal Health Care idea in 1949. But in 1951 when the IRS ruled that employer payments for health insurance were tax-deductible it took the steam out of the movement for Universal Health Care.

In 1965 Lyndon Johnson did manage to get a Medicare bill enacted, health care for the elderly and persons with certain special needs, but healthcare for regular folks was still a non-starter.

Beginning in 1970 bills to enact Universal Health Care of various degrees of coverage were introduced by Republican authors, Democratic authors and authors from both parties acting jointly. Republican President Richard Nixon expressed support for the idea. The effort evolved into more complete Universal coverage plans sponsored by Democrats and more limited proposals sponsored by Republicans working with the AMA. Proposals knocked around for the next 5 years, getting scaled back in their ambitions, before a recession hit and President Ford said he would veto any attempt at Health Care reform.

Candidate Jimmy Carter proposed a Universal Health Care bill in 1976 but once he became President Carter scaled back what he would support to bills making minor changes to the existing private system due to the impact on the Federal budget.

1981 to the Present - Republicans Dominate Policy

Ronald Reagan's election pushed Universal Health Care off the table for a decade. Neither he nor the Republican Senate would support a Universal Health Care bill. Ronald Reagan philosophically reached back to re-adopt the classic Republican idea that government is incompetent, the private sector can do everything better than government and that government has no business messing with the rules for any kind of business - including health care.

Reagan himself was somewhat flexible, he did support changes in the law in 1985 to allow some employees to continue their healthcare coverage after leaving employment. But as the years have gone by Republican's emulating Reagan have become increasingly doctrinaire.

With Bill Clinton's election Universal Health Care was back on the table. Led by Hillary Clinton the administration made Universal Health Care the signature issue of their administration, but could not get a bill passed in the 1993-94 session and thereafter faced a hostile Republican Congress. Universal Health Care bills made no progress for the next 14 years, although in 2004 the GW Bush administration enacted a Medicare Prescription Drug program that paid for prescription drugs for elderly and disabled Americans.

By 2007 it was obvious our system was enormously expensive and not particularly effective. For decades, the cost of healthcare inflated far more rapidly than inflation in general, to the point that by 2007 we were paying twice as much for healthcare per person as do citizens of any other country in the world ($15,000 a year in the US as against about $7,000 per year in the next most expensive countries). Yet there were 30 or 40 countries where people live longer, another 30 or 40 where they had lower infant mortality rates. Based on life expectancy and infant mortality even dirt-poor communist regimes like Cuba provided better health care. Employers, the backbone around which our system was designed, were scrambling to get out from under the constantly inflating health insurance premiums.

In 2009 when Barack Obama took office, although we were in the depths of the Great Recession, the idea of Universal Health Care was back on the table. With a Democratic Congress he managed to enact Obamacare. Obamacare touched off a backlash that is still unfolding. It is clear far more people were covered by health insurance than before Obamacare. Whether the amount of money per person we spend on Health care will fall is not yet clear, nor is the impact on the Federal Budget and National debt.

Appendix E - Control and Housing Policy Detail

1918 to 1932 - Republicans Control

As we have seen the Republicans who controlled policy between 1918 and 1932 carried forward the pro-business philosophy Republicans had relied of for decades, believing government intervention risked more harm that good.

When World War I ended in November of 1918 the Government started demobilizing the vast military created for the war. The demobilization filled the country with young men with some money in their pocket and ambitions to build a life. Owning a home or a farm was a major goal for young folks seeking to build a life. Between 1918 and 1926, the real estate market boomed with folks scrambling to borrow money to buy before prices went up further, so property values skyrocketing beyond the intrinsic value of the properties. This was nothing new to the Republicans controlling policy. Financial collapses had happened pretty regularly in the 50+ years since the Civil War so Congress and President did nothing to address the lack of financial regulation, even though agricultural bank failures began to happen regularly starting in about 1921. Republicans probably aggravated the exuberance in 1923 by creating a special lower tax rate, 12.5%, for Capital Gains which applied to income from selling houses and farms, bringing speculators in on the demand side of the market.

Land prices zoomed up to unsustainable levels then reversed course and began to fall. The housing construction market crashed in 1926. Home loans at this time were generally five-year loans with a big balloon payment at the end and no option to refinance[57], so the foreclosures began slowly. Bank failures escalated dramatically in 1930. Farmers began defaulting on loans as the loan amounts exceeded the current value of the property. By 1934 the value of residential constructions had fallen below where it started in 1918.[58] In 1933 there were more than 1000 new foreclosures every day.[59]

As noted earlier between 1920 and 1932 the nations GDP shrank from 88 billion dollars to 57 billion dollars.

1933 to 1980 - Democratic Policy Dominates

Massive changes in Government Policy began with the arrival of the Roosevelt Administration in early 1933. In 1934 the new Democratic Congress created the Federal Housing Authority (FHA) and Federal Deposit Insurance Corporation (FDIC).[60]

The FDIC was created to address the problem of people losing their savings as banks failed. Understandably people stopped putting their money in banks. Bank deposits were the source of home loan funds and the surviving banks were very reluctant to loan what little money they had. The FDIC created a system where banks self insured one another, backed by the Federal Government, insuring bank deposits to reassure folks that it was safe to put their money back in banks. To further protect banks the FHA set up an insurance plan for the banks to make sure they got repaid on their loans. The modern mortgage market was born as the law also set up lending standards banks had to meet to be insured.

---

[57] https://en.wikipedia.org/wiki/Federal_Housing_Administration
[58] '''
[59] https://www.encyclopedia.com/education/news-and-education-magazines/housing-1929-1941
[60] For more detail on the scope of the events in the Great Depression see wikipedia, for example:
https://en.wikipedia.org/wiki/Federal_Housing_Administration

The plan worked, but slowly, as rebuilding the reserves that banks had available for loans was a slow process. So, in 1938 Congress created the Federal National Mortgage Company - now called Fannie Mae. The purpose of Fannie Mae was to expand the funds available to banks to lend by buying mortgages from the banks. The banks lent money to a buyer, then turned around and sold the mortgage to Fannie Mae and had money to make another loan.[61] These steps set the table for the enormous growth and stability in the housing market after World War II.

In 1954, in the brief two years where Republicans controlled both Congress and the Presidency, the law was amended to bring private investors into Fannie Mae. Then in 1968 Fannie Mae was converted to a publicly traded company by Lyndon Johnson to get the debt off the Government books (presumably to disguise the true cost of the Vietnam war). At this point the parts of Fannie Mae that handled VA loans and Farm Home Loans were spun off into a separate company - the Government National Mortgage Company, dubbed Ginnie Mae.[62] In 1956, 49% of net mortgage financing in the US was insured and guaranteed by the Federal government.[63]

Since after 1968 Fannie Mae was a huge publicly traded, profit oriented monopoly, in 1970 Democrats created Freddie Mac, The Federal Home Loan Mortgage Company, to compete with Fannie Mae. Once

---

[61] https://en.wikipedia.org/wiki/Fannie_Mae

[62] https://en.wikipedia.org/wiki/Government_National_Mortgage_Association

[63] https://books.google.com/books?id=iswRQPyOIgMC&pg=PA62&dq=what+caused+the+postwar+housing+boom&hl=en&sa=X&ved=0ahUKEwi77N7rvrjaAhXLxVQKHWg9AQwQ6AEINzAD#v=onepage&q=what%20caused%20the%20postwar%20housing%20boom&f=false

Republicans took control of policy again Freddie Mac was converted to a for profit business in 1989.

Tax policy also contributed to the long period of housing stability from the 1930's through the 1970's. If you needed to sell your house to move to a new job, or trade up to a bigger house for your family, there were no tax consequences if you put all the proceeds of your sale into buying the new house. This scheme discouraged speculators. Speculators want to make money by buying and selling houses. Since proceeds not rolled into another house were taxed, the profit potential was not an attractive investment unless house prices were increasing far faster than inflation. Since homeowners were not competing with speculators, price rises on housing were modest and foreclosures were relatively rare.

1981 to 2018 - Republican Policy Dominates

From **1981 to 1987** the Reagan revolution domestic agenda focused on reducing regulations and tax cuts and presided over the developing Savings and Loan (S&Ls) crisis. The Savings and Loan banking system had been created and insured by the government in the 1930's as another mechanism to try to get more money available for people to buy homes. The high inflation that peaked around 1980 caused the Federal Reserve to raise the cost banks had to pay to borrow money to the point it cost Savings and Loans more to borrow money than the law, which capped interest, would allow them to recover. In 1979 the Carter Administration and a Democratic Congress allowed S&Ls to raise the interest rates they charged.[64] However the Fed kept pushing rates higher in its efforts to tame

---

[64] Depository Institutions Deregulation and Monetary Control Act of 1980

inflation. In 1982 Congress made amendments eliminating the interest rate cap altogether (which perhaps made sense) but also allowing Savings and Loans to engage in more speculative loans. In effect the law allowed corporations in financial difficulty to gamble with limited liability for their losses. Between 1983 and 1985 S&L assets grew 56% nationally. Then in 1986 S&L's began to fail.[65] Between 1986 and 1995, more than 1000 Savings and Loans Banks went bankrupt.[66]

Ultimately, the Savings and Loan crisis cost the Federal Government about $100 billion to cover depositor (citizen) losses. In the end the crisis was a product of politicians of both parties not being willing to limit Savings and Loan ability to gamble on risky investments.

1987 to 1994 - A quick overview of Republican economic notions at this time can be found in the words of Alan Greenspan, appointed as Chairman of the Federal Reserve in 1987 (serving until 2006). Greenspan summed up his ideology in a 2007 interview:

"Well, I stated that I'm a libertarian Republican, which means I believe in a series of issues, such as smaller government, constraint on budget deficits, free markets, globalization, and a whole series of other things, including welfare reform. And as you may remember, Bill Clinton was pretty much in the same — was doing much that same agenda. And so, I got to consider him as someone — as he described it, we were both an odd couple, because he is a centrist Democrat. And that's not all that far from libertarian Republicanism."[67]

---

[65] https://www.thebalance.com/savings-and-loans-crisis-causes-cost-3306035
[66] https://www.thebalance.com/savings-and-loans-crisis-causes-cost-3306035
[67] http://www.resilience.org/stories/2007-09-25/united-states-sept-25/

So, the Fed kept interest rates low as Republicans lowered taxes and repealed many of the financial restrictions on lending practices put in place after the Great Depression. By the early 2000's you could get a home loan (called a sub-prime loan) with no down payment, no real income and generous terms that didn't require you to come up with money until years down the road. The lenders would make the loan then sell it to someone else, in particular newly deregulated banks like Lehman Brothers. These banks began creating complex securities of bundled loans sold in derivative markets. This derivative market encouraged bankers to bring in as many new loans as possible, regardless of their solvency. As a result, countless sub-prime loans were granted to overeager buyers or speculators who did not have the money to qualify for a traditional mortgage. Freddie Mac and Fannie Mae, at this point for profit entities governed by investors, but guaranteed by government, got blinded by dollar signs and put aside good sense mortgage practices.

In addition, in 1996 the Republican Congress wrote a change in the way Capital Gains on residential property would be computed into a big tax and spending bill. Under the prior law you could sell your house and buy a new one without tax consequences as long as you put the money from the sale of your house into a new personal residence. In its place Congress created a system where if you lived 2 years out of five in any house you could sell it and walk away with hundreds of thousands of profits tax-free. It was a speculator's dream. Buy a house using borrowed money, live in on a couple years, while you fix it up, sell the first house, pay off your loan and walk away with a big tax-free payday. Then start over again with a new house you bought with borrowed money. Within a year at almost any time of day you could find a TV shows about how to flip a house and get rich, a programming niche that was non-existent previously.

The influx of homebuyers and speculators taking advantage of the changes in the tax law, caused the housing market to boom, and the price of an American home increased by 124% between 1998 and 2006.[68] Intentionally, or unintentionally Congress had front loaded the demand side of the housing market. The rate of homeownership increased from 65.9% to 68.5% during this period- the most significant growth spurt since the post-war era (about 1 million new homeowners).[69] Then in the summer of 2006 home values began to fall. As the value of houses fell below the loan amounts loan defaults began. House prices fell 33% after 2006.[70] As more and more people walked away from houses worth less than they owed all the people who bought those complex derivatives found it impossible to sort out who had to take the loss, leading the near paralysis in financial markets. Only the government stepping in to put up trillions of dollars kept the Great Recession from collapsing into another Great Depression.[71]

As part of the response to the Great Recession the Federal Reserve dropped the rate of interest they charge to banks to effectively zero, banks could have money virtually free. Rates have remained near zero for most of the last decade. The historically low interest rates have allowed mortgage loan rates to drop to historically low levels supporting a rebound in the price of houses. Nationally as of early 2018 prices were about 1% higher than in 2006. However, the rise has been uneven, some areas prices have surged far above 2006,

---

[68] https://www.economist.com/node/9972489
[69] https://www.census.gov/housing/hvs/files/currenthvspress.pdf
[70] https://www.corelogic.com/downloadable-docs/corelogic-peak-totrough-final-030118.pdf
[71] https://www.forbes.com/sites/mikecollins/2015/07/14/the-big-bank-bailout/#1ee74d772d83

but 2.5 million mortgages in other areas still owe more than the value of the house.

In many of the markets where the rebound has been most pronounced homeowners are paying a far larger part of their income for housing than folks paid in the past.

As this is being written in 2019 interest rates, and mortgage rates, are going up. Although mortgage rates are still relatively cheap by historical standards in the markets where prices have been most robust there is reason to suspect homeowners already stretched thin to get a loan at 3% will not be able to afford the payment on a loan of 4.5 to 5%. In addition, speculators have played a significant role in the demand that has driven prices up. As speculators see prices stabilize or start to fall they could aggravate a drop out of the market that once again leaves some folks with loans that exceed the value of their house.

The home ownership rate dropped to 62% by 2016 but has since risen to 64.3%. It may be on its way down again.

Appendix F - The Authors Political Background

The scramble for political power is one of the human activities where being competitive and cutthroat may make the difference between success and failure. A functioning Democracy moderates the scramble somewhat, people won't vote for someone who too plainly exhibits an obsession with being in control at all costs. But it is the nature of politics to push folks to use whatever means are available to achieve their goals. One of the means of distinguishing oneself from others is to adopt a partisan ideology and become unwavering your beliefs.

Given our current fiercely partisan political climate, how is the reader to approach this volume? I am prone to ignore writing that appears to be just another partisan hit piece from either the left or the right. So, I must face the possibility this work will face the same dismissive approach.

This volume tries to tiptoe around political partisanship and just develop an understanding of what has happened historically. I don't consider myself a partisan. But, of course, any clever partisan would say the same thing to catch as many eyeballs as possible. So, I provide discussion on this volume and a little detail on my political background to encourage you to read this volume with an open mind.

Underlying Assumptions - The underlying assumption of this volume is that we all mean well. We all honor and accept the notion that life is ultimately about everyone being guaranteed the right to life, liberty and the pursuit of happiness, and that our disagreements aren't about the goal. Disagreements are about the means of achieving that goal.

This volume is rooted in the belief that our goal as individuals should be to live a productive and healthy life, and to insure our individual and family productivity and health we should strive to create a frictionless society where all expect to be responsible for themselves, to the extent they are capable, and all have opportunities and support to achieve life, liberty and the pursuit of happiness.

Like all thinking humans I have biases and motivations under the surface of my conscious thought. I have worked hard over my life to recognize and address bias and motivations that influence my thinking, but it is a constant process to exam your thinking, and life is full of more rewarding ways to spend your time. Work, family - even simply having fun. I recognize I am never able to think without some element of my own background motivations and bias influencing my thoughts. As I wrote every sentence in this volume, I examined my thoughts for unconscious motivations or bias, so I ask that you focus on the data rather than searching for my secret bias.

Non-partisan? - Most partisan hit pieces exploit the fact political affiliations usually have more to do with emotions than data, so seek to exploit emotion. This volume, however, eschews emotion to set out facts widely available on the Internet, footnote sources and compiles and compares different data sets - sort of the (yawn) opposite of playing the emotion card. Despite the probable negative impact on sales, this volume generally bends over backwards to avoid appealing to emotions.

Partisan misrepresentation thrives because we all, the author included, use political affiliations as a shortcut in making political decisions. The world is complicated. To develop the understanding to evaluate political issues would require we devote big chunks of our life to researching and analyzing each issue of the day before we even begin to make an informed decision. Those of us without personal political ambition would generally rather live life than spend the better part of life developing the understanding to evaluate all the complexities of the scores of political issues that present themselves at any given time. We identify with a particular political party with whose creed we are intellectually and/or emotionally comfortable and use that ideological belief to guide our political decision-making.

To help you the reader evaluate my ability to write as a neutral observer here is a summary of my political affiliation background to demonstrate that I have viewed the world from both sides of the partisan divide.

The Authors Political Affiliation History - Like many people I inherited my political beliefs from my family. I grew up as a conservative Republican. My father spoke approvingly on the John Birch Society (although they sometimes were not conservative enough for him). In high school I devoured every word of "A Choice Not an Echo" and "None Dare Call It Treason." I thought we were all doomed to become communists when Lyndon Johnson buried Barry Goldwater in the 1964 Presidential Election.

I might still be a Conservative Republican if my family and I had not been blindsided by a sudden and totally unanticipated family tragedy in April of 1967. My younger brother died suddenly. A couple months later I got drafted. His death left me philosophically comatose with grief for many months.

But being in the Army for the next two years, where what I did and where I did it was dictated by Uncle Sam, gave me the space to think. Once I came out of comatose grief, I came to the conclusion to avoid such overwhelming grief in the future I needed to not take anyone's word for how the world works, or should work. I started my own personal investigation into what was really true.

None of my views changed immediately. But I began a lifetime of thinking about whether the beliefs I was emotionally attached to from childhood really reflected the reality I experienced, an investigation that over time reshaped my thinking.

Politically for the twenty-five years after I first voted in 1968, I flip-flopped back and forth, being registered mostly Republican but for some periods of time as a Democrat, often using ideology as a shortcut for decision making in the voting booth. In the early 1980's I was a registered Republican and voted for President Reagan, but as the Reagan years progressed, I developed doubts about President Reagan's adoption of the trickle-down economics theory. Over the next few years, I grew more disenchanted as Republicans clung to what appeared to me to be an economic policy rooted in wishful thinking.

By this point in my life I was perhaps more acutely aware of Republican's legislative policy decisions as my professional life had moved into developing an expertise in legislative enactments. By the early 1990's I became a registered Democrat and have not since switched.

The Authors Political Views - In my younger years I operated on the rule of thumb that Republicans were right about ⅓ or the time, Democrats were right about ⅓ of the time and they were both wrong about ⅓ of the time. I might change the percentages at this point in my life, but I have been a registered Democrat since 1993 not because I think Democrats have all the answers, but because, despite the explosion in our understanding of how the world works Republicans seem mesmerized by ideological ideas developed in the distant past as solutions to a different world.

I have endeavored to keep my personal views either out of this volume completely, or transparent when my views are unavoidable. I invite you to judge my success. As I am a far from perfect proofreader, I ask that you don't quibble about the occasional minor factual or computational errors. Unless you just want to ignore the big picture, or convince other people to ignore the big picture, then by all means, quibble away.

Perhaps this explanation was is in vain. A clever partisan could have made this all up. Ultimately if you don't know me, you'll have to either trust me or check the sources I cite and the computations I rely on to make sure I am not making it up.

www.ingramcontent.com/pod-product-compliance
Lightning Source LLC
Chambersburg PA
CBHW021820170526
45157CB00007B/2653